Better Homes and Gardens®

YOU CAN
CAN

WILEY

John Wiley & Sons, Inc.

Meredith Corporation

Editor: Jan Miller

Contributing Writer and Editor: Veronica Lorson Fowler, Waterbury Publications, Inc.

Contributing Editor: Lisa Kingsley, Waterbury Publications, Inc.

Contributing Photographers: Marty Baldwin, Jason Donnelly, Robert Jacobs, Scott Little, Kritsada Panichgul

Contributing Food Stylists: Greg Luna, Diana Nolin, Jennifer Peterson, Nicole Peterson, Charles Worthington

John Wiley & Sons, Inc.

Publisher: Natalie Chapman

Associate Publisher: Jessica Goodman

Executive Editor: Anne Ficklen

Editor: Charleen Barila

Production Director: Diana Cisek

Production Editor: Abby Saul

Manufacturing Manager: Tom Hyland

Design Director: Ken Carlson, Waterbury Publications, Inc.

Associate Design Director: Doug Samuelson, Waterbury Publications, Inc.

Production Assistant: Mindy Samuelson, Waterbury Publications, Inc.

Our seal assures you that every recipe in *You Can Can* has been tested in the Better Homes and Gardens® Test Kitchen. This means that each recipe is practical and reliable and meets our high standards of taste appeal. We guarantee your satisfaction with this book for as long as you own it.

CONTENTS

YOU REALLY CAN CAN

IN THE PAST FEW YEARS, canning has experienced a resurgence as a new generation has embraced the concept of gathering beautiful produce from the garden or local farm stand to preserve for enjoyment all year long.

You, too, will enjoy transforming the fat red tomatoes of August into delicious sauces that grace the dinner table in February. Or picking delicate raspberries on a June morning and simmering them into jam to brighten breakfast on the dreariest March day. Or growing cucumbers with care in the garden and preserving them in a tangy brine to make crunchy pickles that evoke the nostalgic flavors of Grandma's table.

Another benefit of canning is decidedly modern: You control the ingredients to fit your lifestyle. Just about everything that goes into your home-canned products can be healthful, natural, and organic, with minimal sugar, salt, or fat.

Canning is also economical, a great way to cut food costs while getting the best for your investment. If you grow your own produce, after the initial investment in jars and equipment, you can serve a variety of full-flavor, top-quality food for pennies.

But the best reason to can may be the emotional element—the deep satisfaction of putting up your own food. Gardening and canning allows you to live with the seasons. It's richly rewarding to set jar after jar of delicious canned foods in a neat row on a pantry or cupboard shelf, storing months of good eating just an arm's reach away.

You Can Can will set you on your way. This book is filled with clear, simple instructions and helpful tips designed with first-time canners in mind. Although the concept of canning can be a little bit intimidating to beginners, it's really very easy. This book offers the safest, simplest, most up-to-the-minute methods to ensure success.

The recipes include tried-and-true favorites, such as Strawberry Jam, Watermelon Pickles, and Applesauce, as well as innovative twists that are sure to please today's more adventurous palates, such as Gingered Cranberry-Pear Chutney, Sweet Jalapeño Slices, and spicy Indian Cauliflower.

So read on. Learn how to can easily and with assurance. Find recipes that inspire you—then gather your produce, get some water boiling, and have fun. (You really can can!)

Chapter One

CANNING BASICS

Welcome to canning! There's a little bit of magic in canning—transforming simple fruits and vegetables into delicious foods that keep for months on a shelf. But there's no mystery. Learn what a simple—and satisfying—process it is with these easy step-by-step directions.

HOW DOES CANNING WORK?

Understanding the fundamentals of canning will set you on your way. Learn a few basics and you're sure to have a safe—and delicious—experience.

Decades ago people canned because they had to. "Putting up" food in crocks and jars was one of the most reliable ways to preserve the bounty of the summer garden.

Today people can because they choose to. They have more control over how the foods are grown and processed—and few things are more satisfying than stepping back from a canning session to admire gleaming jars filled with gorgeous produce.

Over the years the basic process of canning remains the same, however: Heat food to a specified temperature for a particular period of time to destroy harmful microorganisms and inactivate enzymes. The process also vacuum-seals jars to remove air and prevent other micro-organisms from invading.

Microorganisms include molds, yeasts, and bacteria. They are naturally occurring and sometimes even beneficial, such as those found in yogurt. But others are harmful and must be destroyed with heat.

Enzymes are also naturally occurring. They are helpful in nature, but in canning, enzymes can affect the color, texture, and flavor of foods. Heating inactivates these enzymes.

The vacuum seal is a result of heat penetrating the jar in the canner. As food and air in the jar expand with heat, pressure builds in the jar.

After the jars are removed from the canner to cool on the counter, the air cools and contracts, creating a vacuum in the jar, pulling the lid downward into a concave shape. (The metal lids make a popping sound as this happens.) The sticky compound around the rim of the lid, softened by the heat, cools and seals the jar.

The result? A shelf-stable product that can be stored in a pantry or cupboard to enjoy for up to a year.

THE MORE THE MERRIER
Canning can be done solo, but some of the most satisfying canning projects are done with friends and family. Get together a group and speed through the job while sharing a few hours of fun.

Invite them all to bring their own stash of produce. Or make a day of harvesting produce at a pick-your-own farm. At home, turn the harvest into delicious jams, sauces, and more.

THE FIVE RULES OF CANNING
Follow these basic rules to ensure success.

1 KNOW WHICH CANNER TO USE
The boiling-water canner—basically a big pot with a lid and a rack in the bottom—is used for high-acid foods, which naturally resist bacteria growth. Pressure canners are used with low-acid foods and recipes that are especially prone to harboring harmful microorganisms. They heat food hotter than boiling-water canners.

The recipe will specify which type of canner is appropriate. In this book, nearly all the recipes can be made in a boiling-water canner. (See pages 19 and 22 for more information.)

2 CHOOSE THE RIGHT JARS Use jars made specifically for canning. Don't use glass jars from purchased food, even if they look like canning jars. Don't use jars that look different from the canning jars currently on the market. And avoid jars with chipped edges, as that can affect the seal.

Use the size jar specified in the recipe because it takes longer to achieve the critical internal temperature in larger jars. (See page 20 for more information.)

3 USE LIDS PROPERLY Use the special two-piece lids manufactured for canning. Reuse the rings, but do not reuse the lids, which have a special sticky compound that seals the jar.

Don't screw lids on too tightly or they won't create a vacuum seal properly. Heat the lids in very hot but not boiling water or the compound won't seal. Test for sealing on each jar after it has cooled. Press the center of the lid. If the button is depressed and does not make a popping sound, it has sealed properly. (See page 37 for more information.)

4 CHOOSE THE RIGHT RECIPE Modern canning recipes are safer than those from just 20 years ago. Jellies, for example, are no longer sealed with wax but in vacuum-sealed jars. Foods may be processed longer or hotter. Always use tested recipes from reliable, current sources—and follow the recipes exactly. Don't alter ingredients. Alterations can change the acidity and compromise food safety. (See page 16 for more information.)

5 KEEP IT CLEAN AND KEEP IT HOT Keep everything scrupulously clean. Wash and sterilize jars. Pack hot food into hot jars one at a time—not assembly-line style. (See page 35 for more information.)

Pick-your-own farms are an economical way to get plenty of top-quality produce at reasonable prices.

SOURCES FOR PRODUCE

Delicious and economical canned foods start with the source. Consider a variety of sources to secure bushels of fresh, healthful produce to make into jams, pickles, soups, condiments, and more.

YOUR GARDEN Your yard can be one of the best, most bountiful sources for produce for canning. Growing fruits and vegetables requires full sun (at least 8 hours of direct, unfiltered light a day). It's also a good way to make sure your produce is organic, if you choose.

If you don't have the space or adequate sun, rent a community garden plot or garden with a friend at his or her place. Share the work and the bounty.

FARMERS' MARKETS Cities of every size throughout the country have farmers' markets, where local growers sell picked-that-morning produce. Shop on a weekend morning and spend the afternoon canning.

PICK-YOUR-OWN Visit these farms in season to harvest at a reasonable cost. After all, you provide the labor.

Strawberries are by far the most popular produce to purchase at these farms because the berries take large amounts of space to grow. Also popular are apples, peaches, blueberries, raspberries, and pumpkins.

COMMUNITY-SUPPORTED AGRICULTURE Over the last 20 years, Community-Supported Agriculture groups (CSAs) have become popular. Typically consumers purchase shares in a local CSA and in return either pick up or receive a delivery for a set amount of seasonal produce each week throughout the growing season.

Search online for CSAs in your area, or ask at a farmer's market, roadside stand, or local food cooperative.

Canners should talk to a CSA coordinator to find out about availability of larger amounts of certain types of produce for preserving.

GROCERY STORES Supermarkets and local food cooperatives may be sources for produce for preserving too.

Granted, you'll pay top dollar and may have to purchase produce in small, inconvenient packages. But grocery stores may be a good source for less expensive bulk items, such as onions or apples, or for items that aren't locally grown, such as oranges.

KNOW YOUR PRODUCE

Not all tomatoes are created equal. Or cucumbers. Or even grapes. Understand key differences among fruits and vegetables to make sure canning projects turn out perfectly.

UNDAMAGED AND UNBLEMISHED When you put top-quality produce in a jar, you get top-quality product coming out of it. Use produce within a day or two of harvesting or purchasing. Store in the refrigerator if necessary (except for tomatoes).

Discard produce that is diseased, moldy, or insect-damaged, though you can cut out small bruises and spots.

SWEETNESS AND RIPENESS Choose produce that is moderately ripe. Avoid fruit that is overripe or underripe (with the exception of recipes that specify, say, green tomatoes). Fully ripe yet firm fruit has the best, fullest flavor and processes the best.

In some cases recipes specify the ripeness of the fruit—it's that critical. Berries and fruits at the peak of their flavor will mash into the correct consistency and produce the most delicious jams and jellies. Underripe or inferior berries have less flavor and less-ideal texture.

ACIDITY Some fruits and vegetables have higher acid levels than others. Acidic produce is naturally easier to preserve because the acid inhibits the growth of some microorganisms. This is why so many home canning recipes rely on vinegar. It's very acidic. Other recipes call for a small amount of lemon juice to boost acidity. (See page 16 for a chart of produce acidity.)

PECTIN This natural substance occurs in a variety of fruits. It's what causes jams and jellies to gel. Most recipes call for the addition of pectin, but some fruits, such as gooseberries, naturally have so much pectin that adding more isn't necessary.

Underripe fruit is high in pectin; overly ripe fruit is low in pectin. So making preserves with overripe fruit might result in a runny product.

Because the sugar in each recipe interacts with the pectin, do not alter the amount of sugar. If you want low- or no-sugar jams and jellies, follow low- or no-sugar recipes.

THE RIGHT TYPE OF PRODUCE Some varieties or cultivars of produce process better than others, and with better results. Paste-type tomatoes, sometimes called roma or plum tomatoes, are firmer and meatier with fewer seeds and juice than beefsteak or slicing tomatoes. Pickling cucumbers, sometimes called Kirby cucumbers, are firmer and stand up to the brining process better, remaining crisp. Avoid wax coating on produce—it prevents absorption of liquids.

Different grapes have different flavors, juiciness, and pectin levels. Use the grape specified in a recipe whenever possible.

TYPES OF TOMATOES

There are a lot of different varieties of tomatoes out there these days. Growing or buying the right type ensures the best canned foods possible.

❶ PASTE-TYPE Also called roma or plum tomatoes. They are smaller and oblong, with fewer seeds and juice. They're also more meaty, making them the perfect canning tomato.

❷ BEEFSTEAK Also called slicing tomatoes. These are medium-size to large and have a wide variety of colors and patterns. They're great for sandwiches and slicing, but not as good for canning. They produce abundant juice that must be cooked down in sauces, have lots of seeds, and are less meaty.

❸ CHERRY OR GRAPE TOMATOES Wonderful for snacking but too much work for canners. Each tomato would need to be individually peeled.

❹ HEIRLOOM "Heirloom" is a catch-all term that simply means the tomato has been grown for several decades or more. Some paste-type tomatoes are heirloom, as are beefsteak and cherry types. Heirloom tomatoes are prized for their diversity of colors, markings, flavors, and textures. Unless it's a paste-type heirloom, it's not the top choice for canning. Also, some unusually colored tomatoes are unattractive when canned.

❺ GREEN TOMATOES Tomato plants are killed by frost but continue to produce right up until then. In fact, some of the tomatoes on the plant haven't even ripened yet. So these green, unripe tomatoes—which are very firm and tart—can be harvested before the frost and used in recipes specifying them.

❻ TOMATILLOS A contribution from Hispanic culture, tomatillos are not technically tomatoes. Instead they are close relatives of the ground cherry. Tomatillos are small—about the size of a walnut—and are green and very tart. You can substitute green tomatoes, but flavor and texture will be somewhat different.

HIGH-ACID AND LOW-ACID FOODS

In canning, the acidity level of foods is critical. High-acid foods are naturally less likely to harbor harmful microorganisms, while low-acid foods require either more acid or more heat for safe canning.

Foods for canning are basically divided into two groups: low-acid and high-acid.

HIGH-ACID FOODS These are the simplest to process. Their high acidity levels create a difficult environment for microorganisms and enzymes to thrive, so processing them in the lower heat of a boiling-water canner is safe.

High-acid foods have a pH of 4.6 or lower. Nearly all fruits, jams, and jellies are low-acid foods. Lemon juice, lime juice, and vinegar are very acidic. For that reason, most pickles and most salsas are high-acid, even though they may contain foods that are otherwise low-acid, such as green beans and carrots.

LOW-ACID FOODS These foods have a pH greater than 4.6. Most vegetables are low-acid, as are most soups, stews, and

Corn is a low-acid food, so when canned, it must be pressure canned.

Tomatoes are close to neutral acidity. Depending on the recipe, they are canned in a boiling-water canner or a pressure-canner.

meat sauces. Unless large amounts of an acidic food (such as vinegar) are added, these low-acid foods must be processed in the higher heat of a pressure canner.

ACIDITY BOOSTERS Lemon juice and vinegar are highly acidic. They're often added to low-acid foods to control harmful bacteria that can't thrive in acidic environments.

That's why canning recipes for tomatoes, which have a fairly neutral pH, often call

for adding of a teaspoon of lemon juice.

It's also why green beans in a vinegary brine can be processed in a boiling-water canner (which doesn't get as hot and doesn't kill microorganisms as effectively as a pressure canner). Plain green beans, on the other hand, must be processed in the higher heat of a pressure canner.

PROCESS IN BOILING-WATER CANNER

pH Level	Food
1.0 to 1.9	Limes
2.0 to 2.9	Lemons, strawberries
3.0 to 3.9	Gooseberries, rhubarb, pickles, oranges, peaches, sauerkraut, apples, apricots, cherries, plums, blueberries, raspberries, blackberries, pears
4.0 to 4.6	Grapes, most tomato recipes

PROCESS IN PRESSURE CANNER

pH Level	Food
4.7 to 4.9	Green beans, eggplant, some tomato recipes
5.0 to 5.9	Asparagus, carrots, pumpkin, sweet peppers, beets, turnips, sweet potatoes, cucumbers, onions, cauliflower, cabbage, okra, zucchini
6.0 to 7.0	Peas, lima beans, corn, spinach

Rhubarb is a highly acidic food, and can be processed in a boiling-water canner.

② PRESSURE CANNING

③ FREEZING

METHODS OF PRESERVING FOOD

Once you have your hands on all that delicious produce, you'll find that there are several ways to preserve its goodness. Choose the right method to produce the desired results.

The way you process produce depends on the desired result. Should raspberries be made into a rich jam, frozen, or elegantly brandied? Should the tomatoes be made into a rich sauce, frozen whole, or dried?

Here's an overview of basic processing methods:

① BOILING-WATER CANNING A boiling-water canner is simply a very large pot with a rack in the bottom and a lid on the top. Jars are submerged in simmering water for a specified time. They are heated to a temperature of 212°F. This method is used mainly for fruits, pickles, salsa, and other high-acid foods. It's also used for some tomato recipes.

② PRESSURE CANNING A pressure canner has a lid that locks on and a dial that allows you to regulate the steam pressure building up inside by turning the burner heat up or down. The pressurized steam is much hotter than boiling water—pressure canning heats jars to 240°F. This higher heat kills tougher microorganisms that can thrive in low-acid foods, such as green beans, soups, and sauces with meat.

③ FREEZING An easy way to preserve garden produce, freezing preserves texture in a way canning doesn't. Freezing is also easy—just prepare the food and put it into airtight containers or bags and stash them in the freezer!

④ BRINING Merely by marinating some foods in a vinegar-base brine you can preserve them for weeks longer than they would stay fresh otherwise. Simply make the brine, pack into scrupulously clean containers, and store in the refrigerator for the maximum recommended time.

⑤ PRESERVING IN ALCOHOL Alcohol, a disinfectant, kills many harmful bacteria. You can preserve fruit in nothing but alcohol, but it's more flavorful to add spices and other flavorings.

⑥ DRYING Food dries most reliably in a dehydrator, a small electric countertop appliance. But you can also dry foods in the oven with some success, as with dried tomatoes and apples, which intensifies flavor and alters texture.

Food dried in a dehydrator can be safely stored in plastic bags or jars on a shelf. However, food dried in an oven doesn't dehydrate as completely, so it should be stored in plastic bags in a refrigerator.

④ BRINING

⑤ PRESERVING IN ALCOHOL

⑥ DRYING

UNDERSTANDING JARS

Wide-mouth or regular-mouth? Quart or pint? There are many different types of canning jars available, each with its advantages and disadvantages. Choose the right jar for the recipe.

More than ever, home canners have a wide selection of jars from which to choose for food preservation.

Larger jars come as either wide-mouth or regular-mouth. Wide-mouth jars are ideal for packing large pieces, such as whole cucumbers or peaches, into a jar. Regular-mouth jars are fine for recipes that don't have large pieces, such as soups, sauces, and juices.

Recipes often specify jar size. The following jars are the most widely available for home canners:

❶ QUART JARS Use these large jars for any large food, such as whole tomatoes, or for a generous amount of a recipe, such as spaghetti sauce or soup for a crowd. These jars come in both wide-mouth and regular-mouth.

❷ PINT JARS The most versatile jar, this can hold nearly anything—smaller amounts of sauce, vegetables to serve a few people, and larger amounts of jam. These jars come in wide- and regular-mouth.

❸ PLASTIC FREEZER JARS Freezer jam stores well in plastic freezer containers and

WIDE-MOUTH   REGULAR-MOUTH

❶ QUART JAR

❷ PINT JAR

❸ PLASTIC FREEZER JARS

MEASURING HEADSPACE

The amount of headspace is specified by the recipe and is important to ensure that a jar seals properly.

Measure headspace with a ruler or canning tool from the top of the jar to the top of the liquid. It's okay if a little bit of solid food rises above the liquid; it will settle into the liquid over time.

glass jars, but these plastic jars are just the right size, with no danger of cracking in the freezer.

④ **8-OUNCE JELLY JARS** Usually with a quilted or other pattern on the side, these jars have straight sides for better freezing (no shoulders for freezing food to push up and break) and for getting every last bit of jam out of the jar.

⑤ **4-OUNCE JARS** Home-canned food doesn't last as long in the refrigerator as commercial products because no artificial preservatives are added. These small jars hold amounts you'll use up more quickly.

⑥ **DECORATIVE JARS** For refrigerator-pickled foods that don't require heat processing, decorative glass jars work fine.

Just make sure you sterilize them in almost-boiling water before filling.

⑦ **VINTAGE JARS** Old canning jars with colored glass or spring-type lids are pretty collector pieces but they shouldn't be used in modern canning. They have irregular sizes, may crack, and don't seal properly.

⑦ **VINTAGE JARS**

④ **8-OUNCE JELLY JAR**

⑤ **4-OUNCE JAR**

⑥ **DECORATIVE JARS**

CANNING TOOLBOX: CANNERS

The largest and a key piece of equipment in canning is the canner. Here's what you need to know about the two basic types and which one to use for different types of canning.

BOILING-WATER CANNER

This method is also called hot-water canning or a hot water bath. It's used for fruits, tomatoes, salsas, pickles, relishes, jams, and jellies. It's a very simple setup, nothing more than a very large pot with a rack at the bottom on which to set jars.

A boiling-water canner heats jars to 212°F, enough to kill microorganisms found in high-acid foods (see page 16). The rack allows water to flow beneath the jars for even heating. It also has handles that allow you to lower and lift jars easily into the hot water. Canners come in different sizes and finishes. A traditional speckled enamel finish resists chips and rust well. High-end boiling-water canners are available in sleek polished steel.

LID

KETTLE

BOILING-WATER CANNER

PRESSURE REGULATOR — VENT PIPE

SAFETY VALVE

LOCKING LID

GASKET
(BETWEEN LID AND POT)

PRESSURE CANNER

PRESSURE CANNER

This canner is used for most vegetables and other low-acid foods (see page 16). It's also used to process some foods that contain low-acid ingredients, such as most soups and sauces containing meat.

The pressurized steam the canner produces is hotter than boiling water, so it can heat foods to 240°F, hot enough to kill the tougher microorganisms found in low-acid foods. Unlike a boiling-water canner, put only 2 to 3 inches of water into the bottom—don't fill it—because you're creating steam, not a bath of boiling water.

Much safer than pressure canners made years ago, today's pressure canner is also simpler to use. It has a rack in the bottom and a heavy lid that twists and locks in place.

PRESSURE-CANNER REGULATORS

On the top of all pressure canners is a dial or knoblike device—the pressure regulator. It helps you control the pressure inside the canner. There are three types.

ONE-PIECE PRESSURE REGULATOR This is the most common type sold today. Add or remove weight rings from it to set the pressure canner for 5, 10, or 15 pounds. Set the regulator on top of the vent pipe to start the pressurizing process. Adjust heat to control the rattling sound it makes as the canner gains or loses pressure.

DIAL GAUGE REGULATOR More common in older models, a dial regulator shows exact pressure inside the canner. Adjust heat up and down to stay at whatever weight is specified in a recipe. A dial regulator must be inspected for accuracy annually. Your local cooperative extension service or a store that sells pressure canners can advise where to get a dial checked.

WEIGHTED REGULATOR Made of a disklike piece of metal, this must be set on the vent pipe at the correct position to process at 5, 10, or 15 pounds. Like a one-piece pressure regulator, it makes a rocking sound.

USE WHAT YOU HAVE

Today's boiling-water canners are sold with special racks that set the jars submerged in the water or that can be lifted up to rest on the side and hold the jars partially submerged. But you don't have to buy a special boiling-water canner to can. If you have a large stockpot that has a well-fitting lid and holds several jars to a few inches deeper than their height, you can use that instead. However, you'll need a rack to set jars up off the bottom to allow water to flow under them and heat the jars evenly. Make your own rack by wiring together lid rings to fit into the pot.

CANNING TOOLBOX: THE BASICS

Some simple tools make canning—especially of larger amounts of produce—fast and easy with less cleanup. You'll have many of these tools in your kitchen already. But a few specialty canning tools—such as a handy magnet to fish lids out of boiling water with the greatest of ease—make the job much easier.

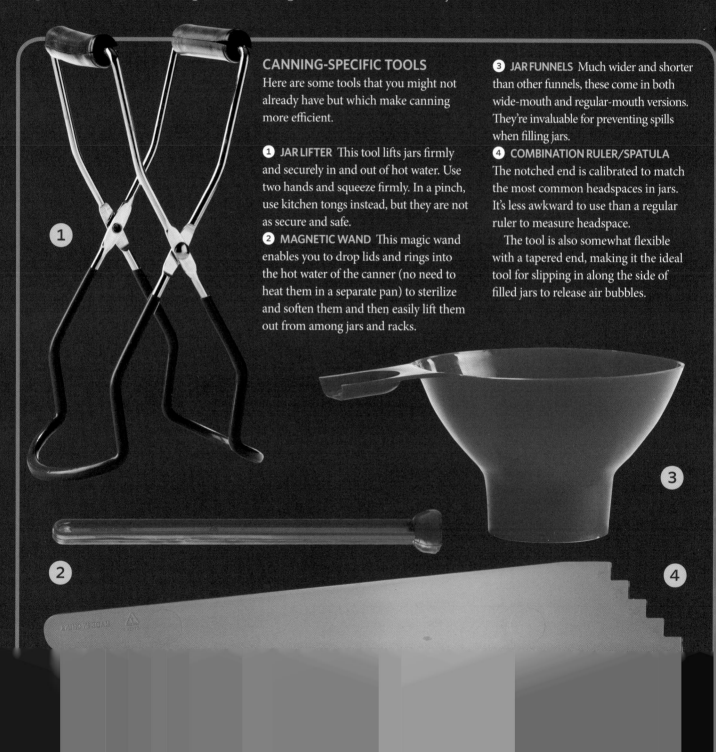

CANNING-SPECIFIC TOOLS

Here are some tools that you might not already have but which make canning more efficient.

1 JAR LIFTER This tool lifts jars firmly and securely in and out of hot water. Use two hands and squeeze firmly. In a pinch, use kitchen tongs instead, but they are not as secure and safe.

2 MAGNETIC WAND This magic wand enables you to drop lids and rings into the hot water of the canner (no need to heat them in a separate pan) to sterilize and soften them and then easily lift them out from among jars and racks.

3 JAR FUNNELS Much wider and shorter than other funnels, these come in both wide-mouth and regular-mouth versions. They're invaluable for preventing spills when filling jars.

4 COMBINATION RULER/SPATULA The notched end is calibrated to match the most common headspaces in jars. It's less awkward to use than a regular ruler to measure headspace.

The tool is also somewhat flexible with a tapered end, making it the ideal tool for slipping in along the side of filled jars to release air bubbles.

ORDINARY KITCHEN TOOLS

These basic kitchen tools are necessary for successful canning.

1 MEASURING SPOONS Most sets have 1 tablespoon, 1 teaspoon, ½ teaspoon, and ¼ teaspoon. Quality metal spoons cost just a bit more and like metal measuring cups better release finely ground foods that might otherwise cling.

2 LADLES Canning involves transferring liquids from one container to another, and a ladle does that quickly and precisely. Metal is ideal because it won't melt if left too close to a burner. If you use plastic, select a black one; light-color plastic tends to stain.

3 RULER Use to measure headspace when filling jars or when a recipe specifies produce cut in certain lengths.

4 MEASURING CUPS Use measuring cups for dry goods, such as sugar. (Use glass measures for liquids; they measure differently.) Metal is more durable and finely ground food slides out of it more easily with no static cling. Most come in sets of 1 cup, ½ cup, ⅓ cup, and ¼ cup.

5 KITCHEN TOWELS These have many uses when canning, besides drying wet utensils. Use to wipe rims of jars. Lay a dry towel on the counter to set hot jars on (never directly on the counter; they may crack) or set on a wire rack. And, of course, use them to wipe up spills.

6 TIMER A timer is important for keeping track of cooking and processing times. The timer built into a stove works fine, but a portable timer can be tucked in your pocket while you leave the room.

7 HOT PADS One pair is essential, but two is better so that you always have a clean, dry pair (wet hot pads conduct heat, resulting in burns). Or try silicone hot pads—they clean up in a snap.

8 COLANDER Useful for washing produce and draining juice from sliced or cut-up produce. Line it with cheesecloth and set over a bowl to finely strain juices for canned juice or jellies.

9 LARGE SIEVE Use this like a small colander. Rinse off small amounts of berries or set over a bowl to strain bits from liquids. Or line with cheesecloth to finely strain small amounts of liquid.

10 PERMANENT MARKER Use to write on metal, paper, plastic, and glass. Once the ink is dry, it is fairly resistant to fading and moisture.

11 8-CUP LIQUID MEASURING JAR Essential for measuring large amounts of chopped or sliced produce and for measuring large amounts of water and other liquids. It also makes a handy mixing bowl.

1 ASCORBIC ACID
COLOR KEEPER

2 SALT

3 SUGAR

4 PICKLING LIME

5 PECTIN

6 VINEGAR

7 BOTTLED
LEMON JUICE

UNDERSTANDING CANNING INGREDIENTS

Canning uses some specialty ingredients that improve the quality (and, in some cases, safety) of food. Some are as basic as salt—others are more specialized.

Most ingredients for canning are already in your pantry—that's the beauty of home preservation. You aren't using chemicals or additives whose names you can't pronounce and that you don't understand.

That doesn't mean each ingredient isn't important. Each has its role in the canning process, interacting with other ingredients, so don't vary or substitute unless the recipe specifies. A few key specialty ingredients that help ensure quality canned goods:

1 ASCORBIC ACID COLOR KEEPER This powder protects color and flavor of fruits, such as apples and peaches, and vegetables that darken when peeled or cut.

Dissolve the powder in water. Then briefly soak cut-up produce in the solution.

2 SALT A variety of salts can be used in canning recipes, but for best results use canning salt. It has a fine texture and will dissolve readily. Its fine texture also makes it measure differently than coarser salts, so use it for the most accurate measuring in canning recipes. Also, canning salt is free from anticlumping additives that can cause cloudiness in brines.

Salt is one of the few ingredients in canning that you can adjust in all recipes to taste.

3 SUGAR Sugar, obviously, helps flavor foods. However, when simmered, it also affects the texture of canned goods, making them thicker. Sugar interacts with pectin, so follow any recipe that calls for both exactly to avoid a preserve that's too thick or too runny. Do not substitute honey unless the recipe specifies it.

4 PICKLING LIME Not to be confused with the citrus fruit lime, this powder is made of calcium hydroxide, which improves firmness in pickles. Dissolve the powder in water and soak produce (usually cucumbers) in it for a day or two. Rinse thoroughly several times with repeat soakings to remove excess lime. Use only in recipes that specify its use.

5 PECTIN Available in a variety of formulations, pectin adds body and gel to jams and jellies. Use traditional powder types by first mixing them with sugar, then mixing them with the fruit and other ingredients. Stir or cook fruit to dissolve the pectin.

Liquid pectin speeds the dissolving process. Use low-sugar pectins to reduce sugar in jams and preserves. (Follow a low-sugar recipe or follow the directions on the product; don't just reduce the sugar, or texture will be affected.)

Freezer-jam pectins dissolve quickly and create optimal texture in freezer preserves, which tend to be slightly softer than traditional preserves.

6 VINEGAR This highly acidic liquid is key to making pickles, salsas, and other preserved goods. Recipes usually specify what type of vinegar to use. However, when in doubt, use white vinegar, which you can purchase by the gallon, because it's clear and won't discolor produce.

Apple cider vinegar is also commonly used in canning recipes.

7 BOTTLED LEMON JUICE Fresh lemon juice and grated lemon peel are added to some recipes for flavor. But in other recipes (such as those containing tomatoes) that call for lemon juice, use only bottled lemon juice.

In those recipes, lemon juice is added to boost acidity for a safe product. Use bottled lemon juice because it has consistent acidity, unlike that of fresh lemons, which vary in acidity.

FOLLOW THE RECIPE

A good canning recipe has been carefully tested to make sure that the combination of ingredients works together for a safe, high-quality product. Do not reduce or increase the amount of any ingredient, except for dried herbs and salt.

Don't add or eliminate any ingredients. Even something as simple as the addition or substitution of fresh herbs can alter the pH of the recipe enough to affect its safety.

HOW TO PREP PRODUCE

Before making pickles, preserves, or any other type of canned produce, some simple preparation of the produce is necessary. Here's how to prep even large amounts of fruits and vegetables like a pro.

With any canning recipe, it's important to first prepare produce.

First wash the produce. Use only water, rinsing thoroughly. (A large colander is useful for this process.) Washing removes dirt, insects, and bacteria. Use a scrubber brush to get dirt off rough root vegetables such as carrots.

Peel the produce only if the recipe specifies it. Some peels are left on because they contain valuable pectin, which helps thicken the product. In other cases the peel helps keep the produce intact.

Some recipes specify blanching—simply putting produce into rapidly boiling water for a short time, usually a minute or two.

Blanching, most often called for in freezing recipes, further cleans produce and kills some organisms on the surface. It also slows or stops the action of enzymes, which cause loss of flavor, color, and texture. Blanching also helps preserve color and vitamin content.

For peaches, tomatoes, and some other soft-fleshed produce, blanching makes peeling easy (see page 29). Hot water heats and softens the flesh right beneath the skin. Plunging the produce in cold water causes steam, which cools and leaves tiny air pockets that allow the skin to slip off easily.

(see page 29)

> ## STORING PRODUCE
>
> For canning, use only produce that is at its peak of ripeness and flavor. Purchased produce and home-grown produce should be used within a few days, depending on the fruit or vegetable. Pickling cucumbers and raspberries can wither or mildew in just a day or two.
>
> Store most produce (except for tomatoes) in the refrigerator to slow deterioration. Chilling lessens their flavor. Store tomatoes in a woven basket or spread in a single layer on newspaper until ready to use. This encourages airflow that prevents rotting.

TOMATOES Make an X at the blossom end of a tomato, then blanch. The X encourages the tomato skin to split so that you can slip off the skin easily with your fingers.

STRAWBERRIES Cut out the stem end of strawberries with a small sharp knife. This process is called hulling.

APPLES Make processing apples a breeze by investing a few dollars in an apple corer. Simply push it firmly into the apple, twist, and pull.

HOW TO PEEL PEACHES AND TOMATOES

Blanching produce loosens the skin, making peeling a snap.

1 Bring a large pan of water to boiling. Add the produce and leave in for 30 to 60 seconds or until skins start to split.

2 Remove and plunge produce into a large bowl of ice water. Remove from the cold water after a few minutes. Use a knife to easily pull off the skin.

With the raw-pack method, raw food is put into a hot, sterilized jar and topped with a hot liquid, such as water.

RAW AND HOT PACKS

Food is loaded into jars in one of two ways—the hot-pack or the raw-pack method. Here's how to determine which is better for your situation.

To achieve ideal flavor and texture, a recipe will follow either a hot-pack or raw-pack method.

Although the recipe might not refer to these names, it will instruct you to put food into a jar raw and top it with hot liquid or to cook the food first and pack it, still hot, into jars. With some foods, such as green beans or peaches, a recipe recommends both methods.

HOT PACK

For food that is firm and processes well, this method is preferred. It's the best method for most vegetables, meats, poultry, seafoods, and most fruits.

Simmer food in brine, water, juice, or syrup for a few minutes. Then load the food, still hot, into hot, sterilized jars.

Precooking the food this way breaks it down more to eliminate air so it's less likely to spoil and so food doesn't float. Also more produce can be loaded into fewer jars and processing time is less because the food is already hot—a significant advantage if you're processing large amounts of food.

RAW PACK

Also called cold pack, this method is better for foods that are more delicate and that would have a tough time standing up to a cooking process followed by the heat-intensive canning process.

Food is placed into the jar while still raw and packed in firmly but not crushed. Boiling brine, syrup, juice, or water is added if additional liquid is needed (the recipe will specify).

This method is fast and easy and helps preserve texture. However, it also may result in some shrinkage as food is processed, causing some foods to float to the top of the jar.

ADDING SYRUPS

Some canned fruit recipes call for the addition of syrup.

Generally, heavy syrups, which have more sugar, are used with sour fruits. Light syrups are ideal for sweeter fruits. Also, if you want to cut down on sugar, make a light syrup or even pack in juice or water.

To prepare a syrup, place the following amounts of sugar and water in a large saucepan. Heat until sugar is dissolved. Skim off foam, if it forms, to ensure a clearer syrup. Use syrup hot for canned fruits; chilled for frozen fruits. Allow $1/2$ to $2/3$ cup syrup for each 2 cups fruit.

VERY THIN OR VERY LIGHT SYRUP Dissolve 1 cup sugar with 4 cups water to yield 4 cups syrup.

THIN OR LIGHT SYRUP Dissolve $1 2/3$ cups sugar with 4 cups water to yield $4 1/4$ cups syrup.

MEDIUM SYRUP Use $2 2/3$ cups sugar and 4 cups water to yield $4 2/3$ cups syrup.

HEAVY SYRUP Use 4 cups sugar and 4 cups water to yield $5 3/4$ cups syrup.

With the hot-pack method, food is simmered and then ladled, still hot, into hot jars.

PREPARING JARS AND LIDS

Before filling, jars and lids need to be heated and sterilized in the canner or other hot water to ensure safely canned foods. The process isn't difficult, but follow these directions to do it correctly in record time.

STERILIZING JARS

All jars must be cleaned and sterilized before using.

You can simply dip them in a large pan of simmering water for a few minutes and then load them, still hot, with food.

A more efficient way is to use the canner, which already has hot water in it. After filling the canner halfway and bringing the water to just below a simmer, put the jars in it, filling each jar with some hot water to prevent floating. If the canner has an adjustable rack, position it in the highest position. Cover with the lid to get the jars hot and steamy. They don't need to be submerged; the steam will sterilize them. After a few minutes, the jars are ready to fill.

Take out just one jar at a time, fill it, put on the lid, and return it to the canner to keep everything hot. Then take out another jar and fill it: One jar out, one jar in.

If using a pressure canner, fill the canner with 2 to 3 inches of water and, with the lid loosely (not locked) in place, bring the water to not quite a simmer. Put the jars in the canner with a little water to prevent them from floating.

Put the lid back on—loosely, not locked—and allow the jars to get steamy hot. After a few minutes they will be sterilized and ready to pack with hot food.

Again, take one jar out, fill it, and replace it in the canner before removing another jar: One jar out, one jar in.

HEATING LIDS

Before using lids, heat them to soften the sealing compound. Put the lids in the canner with the jars as you sterilize them.

Lids can be heated in hot (not boiling) water right in the canner. Lift out with a magnetic canning lid wand or tongs.

Or heat them in a saucepan by themselves, if you wish.

Regardless, the water must be very hot (180°F) to soften the compound but must *not* boil or the compound will start to break down.

Rings can be sterilized, too, but it's not necessary. Instead you can wash them in hot, soapy water and rinse thoroughly.

CHOOSING THE LIDS

Lids are essentially flat disks of metal with a sticky compound around the edge. When heated, that compound softens, then cools, and creates a long-lasting seal.

Lids also have a raised circle in the center. After canning, if a vacuum seal has been created, that raised circle is sucked down and flattened. If the seal has not been properly created, you can press the circle with your finger and it will pop up and down. (In that case, refrigerate and eat the food within a few to several days.)

The function of bands is simply to hold the lids in place during processing and cooling. They can be reused many times unless they start to rust.

Sterilize clean jars in hot water right in the canner. Then fill them and replace them into the already-heated water to complete processing.

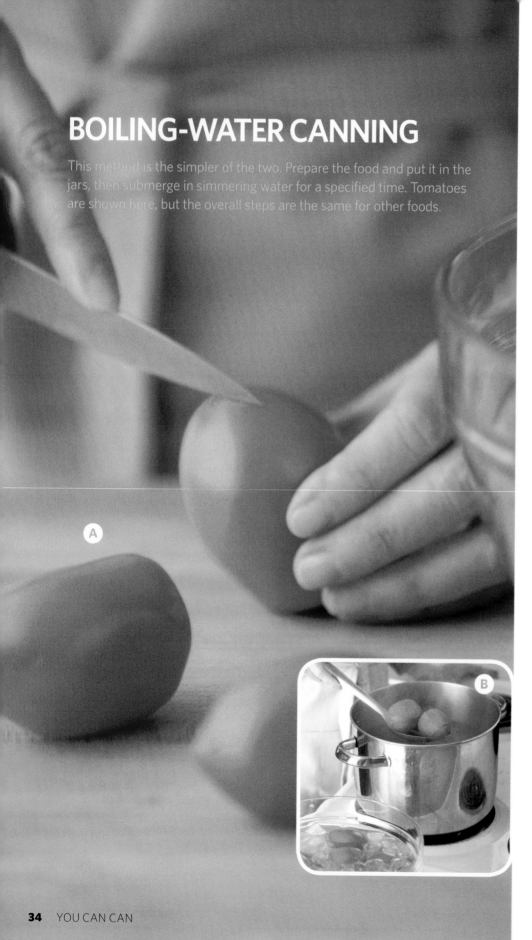

BOILING-WATER CANNING

This method is the simpler of the two. Prepare the food and put it in the jars, then submerge in simmering water for a specified time. Tomatoes are shown here, but the overall steps are the same for other foods.

STEP 1 PREPARE THE FOOD

While you're preparing the food to be canned, heat water in the canner. Fill the canner about halfway with water and position the rack. Set jars in the canner to sterilize (see page 32).

A SCORE THE TOMATOES Make an X in the blossom end of each tomato with a small sharp knife.

B BLANCH Heat a large kettle of water to boiling. Drop in the tomatoes to simmer for 1 or 2 minutes.

C COOL AND PEEL Immediately plunge the tomatoes into icy water to loosen the skins. The skins will slip off easily. Cut out the stem ends with a small, sharp knife.

STEP 2 FILL THE JARS

The cold-pack method for tomatoes is shown here (recipe on page 50), but follow the exact process specified in your recipe.

Ⓐ FILL Pack the jar as tightly as you can with the food without crushing it. Top with any hot liquid as specified in the recipe.

Ⓑ REMOVE AIR BUBBLES Insert a special canning tool or a thin, flexible spatula down along the sides of the jar to remove any air bubbles. Measure headspace (see page 21), adding or removing liquid as needed.

Ⓒ WIPE Wipe rim and threads of jar with a clean, damp cloth to remove any residue that might interfere with the seal.

Ⓓ PUT ON LID Set lid on jar and screw on band no more than fingertip-tight, just tight enough that you could turn the band another ¼ to ½ inch tighter. This is important for a proper seal.

STEP 3 PROCESS THE JARS
Submerging the jars in boiling water heats and sterilizes the food inside and is the first step in creating a sealed jar.

Ⓐ PLACE JARS IN CANNER As you fill each jar, set it back in the canner filled with simmering water. The canner shown has a rack with handles to hang on the canner rim so that jars sit halfway in the water.

Ⓑ PROCESS JARS When all jars are filled, lower them into the canner. They should be covered with 1 to 2 inches water. Add more boiling water if needed to achieve this. Start processing time from the moment the water starts to boil. Keep at a low, rolling boil.

Ⓒ REMOVE JARS When the processing time is up, turn off heat. Using pot holders, lift up the rack and rest handles on the side of the canner. Allow the jars to cool in place for a few minutes.

STEP 4 **COOL** Remove jars from canner and set on a wire rack or towel on the countertop (cold, bare countertops can crack jars). Do not tighten bands. Allow to cool 12 to 24 hours. After that time test the seal by firmly pressing your finger on the center of the lid. It should not give. If it makes a popping sound, it is not properly sealed. Store in the refrigerator and eat the food soon. Otherwise, store jars in a cool, dry place for up to one year.

PRESSURE CANNING

Some foods are low-acid and require the more intense heat created in a pressure canner. Green beans are one such food, but the steps shown here are the same as for other pressure-canned foods.

STEP 1 PREPARE THE FOOD

While you prepare the food, heat 2 or 3 inches of water in the pressure canner with the lid set on it loosely. Set the jars in the canner to sterilize (see page 32) but do **not** lock the lid in place or pressure will start to build.

A WASH AND TRIM Wash the beans. Then cut off and discard the woody stems. Cut off the entire "tail" end of the bean, if desired, but it's not necessary.

B CUT THE BEANS Cut or snip the beans into bite-size sections. Shorter pieces will fit into the jar more easily and make them easier to eat.

STEP 2 FILL THE JARS

The hot-pack method for green beans is shown (see page 31), but the process is similar for other foods that are to be pressure-canned.

A FILL WITH PRODUCE Remove one hot jar at a time from the canner. Fill with the food, using a funnel as needed to keep jar rims clean. Pack in the produce with your fingers as tightly as you can without crushing it. Fill one hot, sterilized jar at a time; do not fill a cooled jar.

B ADD HOT LIQUID Top with boiling water, brine, or other hot liquid as specified in the recipe. Measure headspace (see page 21) as the recipe directs. Add or remove liquid as needed.

C REMOVE AIR BUBBLES Use a thin, flexible spatula or canning tool to remove air bubbles. Add more water if needed to achieve the correct headspace.

D PUT ON LID Wipe off the jar rim and threads with a clean cloth. Set lid in place and screw band on fingertip-tight, just ¼ to ½ inch from very tight. This is important so air can escape for a proper seal. Place the jar back in the canner before filling the next jar.

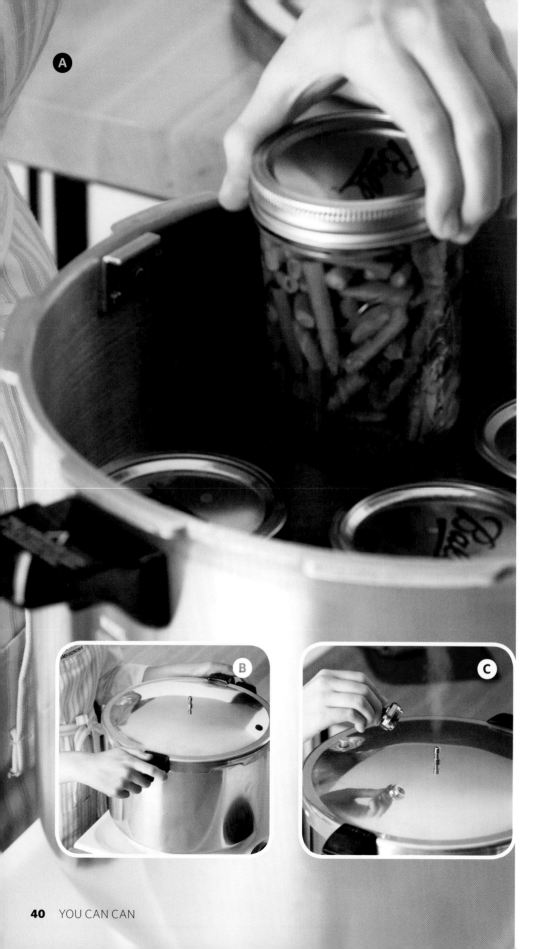

STEP 3 PROCESS When all the jars are filled, close the canner and allow pressure to build. Follow canner directions for your specific model.

Ⓐ FILL THE CANNER Set the last jar in place. The water in the canner should come up only a few inches and not cover the jars. Only enough water to create steam is needed.

Ⓑ LOCK THE LID Set the lid in place and twist so the handles lock it in place. Do not put on the pressure regulator yet.

Ⓒ VENT THE CANNER Turn heat to high and allow a full head of steam to come out of the vent pipe. Allow to vent for 10 minutes. Adjust weights on the pressure regulator as specified in the recipe. Set the pressure regulator on the vent pipe to plug it.

Ⓓ ACHIEVE THE CORRECT PRESSURE The safety valve will pop from the down position to the up position, showing that the canner is now pressurized. Do not open the canner. When the pressure regulator starts to rock, adjust heat so it makes a steady rattling sound. Set the timer for the time specified in the recipe.

STEP 4 COOL THE JARS

Once processing is complete, allow the canner to depressurize and then cool the jars.

A DEPRESSURIZE When the timer goes off, turn off the heat. Do not open the lid. Wait until the safety valve drops back down. This shows that the canner is no longer pressurized and is safe to open.

B OPEN THE CANNER Remove the pressure regulator. (Very little or no steam should escape.) Unlock the handles and open the canner away from you so that steam is directed away from you.

C COOL THE JARS Allow the jars to stand in the canner for 10 minutes to cool slightly. Remove them from the canner and set on a wire rack or dry towel on the countertop. Do not tighten lids. Allow to cool for 12 to 24 hours. Test seals by pressing on the lid (it should not pop up or down). Refrigerate any improperly sealed food to eat soon. Store others in a cool, dry place.

CANNING AND FREEZING VEGETABLES

To clean vegetables prior to processing, wash fresh vegetables with cool, clear tap water; scrub firm vegetables with a clean produce brush to remove any dirt.

VEGETABLE	PREPARATION	PRESSURE CANNING, RAW PACK (See page 31.) *	PRESSURE CANNING, HOT PACK (See page 31.) *	FREEZING
ASPARAGUS	Allow 2½ to 4½ pounds per quart. Wash; scrape off scales. Break off woody bases where spears snap easily; wash again. Sort by thickness. Leave whole or cut into 1-inch lengths.	Not recommended	Not recommended	Blanch small spears for 2 minutes, medium for 3 minutes, and large for 4 minutes; cool quickly by plunging into ice water; drain. Fill containers; shake down, leaving no headspace.
BEANS: BUTTER OR LIMA	Allow 3 to 5 pounds unshelled beans per quart. Wash, shell, rinse, drain, and sort beans by size.	Fill jars with beans; do not shake down. Add boiling water, leaving a 1-inch headspace for pints, 1¼-inch for large beans in quarts, and 1½-inch for small beans in quarts. Process pints for 40 minutes and quarts for 50 minutes.	Cover beans with boiling water; return to boiling. Boil for 3 minutes. Fill jars loosely with beans and cooking liquid, leaving a 1-inch headspace. Process pints for 40 minutes and quarts for 50 minutes.	Blanch small beans for 2 minutes, medium beans for 3 minutes, and large beans for 4 minutes; cool quickly by plunging into ice water; drain. Fill containers loosely, leaving a ½-inch headspace.
BEANS: GREEN, ITALIAN, SNAP, OR WAX (See also pages 38 and 56.)	Allow 1½ to 2½ pounds per quart. Wash; remove ends and strings. Leave whole or cut into 1-inch pieces.	Pack beans tightly in jars; add boiling water, leaving a 1-inch headspace. Process pints for 20 minutes and quarts for 25 minutes.	Cover beans with boiling water; return water to boiling. Boil for 5 minutes. Loosely fill jars with beans and cooking liquid, leaving a 1-inch headspace. Process pints for 20 minutes and quarts for 25 minutes.	Blanch for 3 minutes; cool quickly by plunging into ice water; drain. Fill containers; shake down, leaving a ½-inch headspace.
BEETS (See also page 58.)	Allow 3 pounds (without tops) per quart. Trim off beet tops, leaving 1 inch of stem and roots to reduce bleeding of color. Scrub well. Cover with boiling water. Boil about 15 minutes or until skins slip off easily; cool. Peel; remove stem and roots. Leave baby beets whole. Cut medium or large beets into ½-inch cubes or slices. Halve or quarter large slices.	Not recommended	Pack hot jars to 1 inch from the top with beets. Cover beets with boiling water, leaving 1-inch headspace. Process pints for 30 minutes and quarts for 35 minutes.	Cook unpeeled beets in boiling water until tender. (Allow 25 to 30 minutes for small beets, 45 to 50 minutes for medium beets.) Cool quickly by plunging into ice water; drain. Peel; remove stem and roots. Cut into slices or cubes. Fill containers, leaving a ½-inch headspace.
CARROTS	Use 1- to 1¼-inch diameter carrots (larger carrots may be too fibrous). Allow 2 to 3 pounds per quart. Wash, trim, peel, and rinse again. Leave tiny ones whole; slice or dice larger carrots.	Fill jar tightly to 1 inch from the top with raw carrots. Add boiling water, leaving a 1-inch headspace. Remove air bubbles. Process pints for 25 minutes and quarts for 30 minutes.	Cover carrots with boiling water; return water to boiling. Reduce heat; simmer for 5 minutes. Fill jars with carrots and cooking liquid, leaving a 1-inch headspace. Process pints for 25 minutes and quarts for 30 minutes.	Blanch tiny whole carrots for 5 minutes and cut-up carrots for 2 minutes; cool quickly by plunging into ice water; drain. Pack tightly into containers, leaving a ½-inch headspace.

VEGETABLE	PREPARATION	PRESSURE CANNING, RAW PACK (See page 31.)*	PRESSURE CANNING, HOT PACK (See page 31.)*	FREEZING
CORN, WHOLE KERNEL	Allow 4 to 5 pounds per quart. Remove husks. Scrub with a vegetable brush to remove silks. Wash and drain.	Cover ears with boiling water; boil 3 minutes. Cut corn from cobs at three-quarters depth of kernels; do not scrape. Pack loosely in jars (do not shake or press down). Add boiling water, leaving a 1-inch headspace. Process pints for 55 minutes and quarts for 85 minutes.	Cover ears with boiling water; return to boiling and boil 3 minutes. Cut corn from cobs at three-quarters depth of kernels; do not scrape. Bring to boiling 1 cup water for each 4 cups corn. Add corn; simmer 5 minutes. Fill jars with corn and liquid, leaving a 1-inch headspace. Process pints for 55 minutes and quarts for 85 minutes.	Cover ears with boiling water; return to boiling and boil 4 minutes. Cool by plunging into ice water; drain. Cut corn from cobs at two-thirds depth of kernels; do not scrape. Fill containers, leaving a ½-inch headspace.
PEAS, EDIBLE PODS	Wash Chinese, snow, sugar, or sugar snap peas. Remove stems, blossom ends, and any strings.	Not recommended	Not recommended	Blanch small pods 1½ minutes or large pods 2 minutes. (If peas have started to develop, blanch 3 minutes.) Cool quickly by plunging into ice water; drain. Fill containers, leaving a ½-inch headspace.
PEPPERS, HOT (See also page 104.)	Select firm jalapeño or other chile peppers; wash. Halve large peppers. Remove stems, seeds, and membranes. Place, cut sides down, on a foil-lined baking sheet. Bake in a 425°F oven for 20 to 25 minutes or until skins are bubbly and brown. Cover peppers or wrap in foil and let stand about 15 minutes or until cool. With a paring knife, pull the skin off gently and slowly.	Not recommended	Pack peppers in pint jars. Add boiling water, leaving a 1-inch headspace. Process pints for 35 minutes.	Package in freezer containers, leaving no headspace.
PEPPERS, SWEET (See also page 98.)	Select firm green, bright red, or yellow peppers; wash. Remove stems, seeds, and membranes. Place, cut sides down, on a foil-lined baking sheet. Bake in a 425°F oven for 20 to 25 minutes or until skins are bubbly and brown. Cover peppers or wrap in foil and let stand about 15 minutes or until cool. With a paring knife, pull the skin off gently and slowly.	Not recommended	Quarter large pepper pieces or cut into strips. Loosely pack pint jars to 1 inch from the top. Add boiling water, leaving a 1-inch headspace. Process pints for 35 minutes.	Quarter large pepper pieces or cut into strips. Fill containers, leaving a ½-inch headspace. Or spread peppers in a single layer on a baking sheet; freeze until firm. Fill container, shaking to pack closely and leaving no headspace.

*For a dial-gauge canner, use 11 pounds of pressure; for a weighted-gauge canner, use 10 pounds of pressure. At altitudes above 1,000 feet, see tip, page 191.
NOTE: Add salt, if desired: ¼ to ½ teaspoon for pints and ½ to 1 teaspoon for quarts.

CANNING AND FREEZING FRUITS

Wash fresh fruits with cool, clear tap water but do not soak them; drain. Follow preparation directions. If you choose can or freeze fruits with syrup, select the syrup that best suits the fruit and your taste. See page 31 for directions on making syrups. When freezing an unsweetened pack, leave ½-inch headspace unless otherwise directed. When freezing a sugar, sugar-syrup, or water pack and wide-top containers with straight or slightly flared sides, leave a ½-inch headspace for pints and a 1-inch headspace for quarts. For narrow-top containers and freezing jars, leave a ¾-inch headspace for pints and 1½-inch headspace for quarts.

FOOD	PREPARATION	BOILING-WATER CANNING, RAW PACK	BOILING-WATER CANNING, HOT PACK	FREEZING
APPLES (See also pages 66, 68, and 76.)	Allow 2 to 3 pounds per quart. Select varieties that are crisp, not mealy, in texture. Peel and core; halve, quarter, or slice. Dip into ascorbic acid color keeper solution; drain.	Not recommended	Simmer in syrup for 5 minutes, stirring occasionally. Fill jars with fruit and syrup, leaving a ½-inch headspace. Process pints and quarts for 20 minutes.	Use a syrup, sugar, or unsweetened pack, leaving the recommended headspace.
APRICOTS	Allow 2 to 2½ pounds per quart. If desired, peel (see Peaches, Nectarines, *below*). Prepare as for Peaches, Nectarines. Quality is better when apricots are canned rather than frozen.	See Peaches, Nectarines, *below*.	See Peaches, Nectarines, *below*.	Peel as for peaches, *below*. Use a syrup, sugar, or water pack, leaving the recommended headspace.
BERRIES	Allow 1 to 3 pounds per quart. Can or freeze blackberries, blueberries, currants, elderberries, gooseberries, huckleberries, loganberries, and mulberries. Freeze (do not can) boysenberries, raspberries, and strawberries.	Fill jars with blackberries, loganberries, or mulberries. Shake down gently. Add boiling syrup, leaving a ½-inch headspace. Process pints for 15 minutes and quarts for 20 minutes.	Simmer blueberries, currants, elderberries, gooseberries, and huckleberries in water for 30 seconds; drain. Fill jars with berries and hot syrup, leaving a ½-inch headspace. Process pints and quarts for 15 minutes.	Slice strawberries, if desired. Use a syrup, sugar, or unsweetened pack, leaving the recommended headspace.
CHERRIES	Allow 2 to 3 pounds per quart. If desired, treat with ascorbic acid color-keeper solution; drain. If unpitted, prick skin on opposite sides to prevent splitting.	Fill jars, shaking down gently. Add boiling syrup or water, leaving a ½-inch headspace. Process pints and quarts for 25 minutes.	Add cherries to hot syrup; bring to boiling. Fill jars with fruit and syrup, leaving a ½-inch headspace. Process pints for 15 minutes and quarts for 20 minutes.	Use a syrup, sugar, or unsweetened pack, leaving the recommended headspace.
MELONS	Allow about 4 pounds per quart for cantaloupe, honeydew, and watermelon. Peel and cut into ½-inch cubes or balls.	Not recommended	Not recommended	Use a syrup or unsweetened pack), leaving the recommended headspace.
PEACHES, NECTARINES (See also page 82.)	Allow 2 to 3 pounds per quart. To peel peaches (peeling nectarines is not necessary), immerse in boiling water for 30 to 60 seconds or until skins start to split; remove and plunge into cold water. Halve and pit. If desired, slice. Treat with ascorbic acid color keeper solution; drain.	Fill jars, placing fruit cut sides down. Add boiling syrup or water, leaving a ½-inch headspace. Process pints for 25 minutes and quarts for 30 minutes. Do not raw pack apricots. (Note: Hot packing generally results in a better product.)	Add fruit to hot syrup; bring to boiling. Fill jars with fruit (placing cut sides down) and syrup, leaving a ½-inch headspace. Process pints for 20 minutes and quarts for 25 minutes.	Use a syrup, sugar, or water pack, leaving the recommended headspace.
PEARS (See also pages 70 and 72.)	Allow 2 to 3 pounds per quart. Peel, halve, and core. Treat with ascorbic acid color keeper solution; drain.	Not recommended	Simmer fruit in syrup for 5 minutes. Fill jars with fruit and syrup, leaving a ½-inch headspace. Process pints for 20 minutes and quarts for 25 minutes.	Use a syrup pack, leaving the recommended headspace.

FOOD	PREPARATION	BOILING-WATER CANNING, RAW PACK	BOILING-WATER CANNING, HOT PACK	FREEZING
PLUMS	Allow 1 to 2 pounds per quart. Prick skin on 2 sides. Freestone varieties may be halved and pitted.	Pack firmly into jars. Add boiling syrup, leaving a ½-inch headspace. Process pints for 20 minutes and quarts for 25 minutes.	Simmer in water or syrup for 2 minutes. Remove from heat. Let stand, covered, for 20 to 30 minutes. Fill jars with fruit and cooking liquid or syrup, leaving a ½-inch headspace. Process pints for 20 minutes and quarts for 25 minutes.	Halve and pit. Treat with ascorbic acid color-keeper solution; drain well. Use a syrup pack, leaving the recommended headspace.
RHUBARB (See also page 150.)	Allow 1½ pounds per quart. Discard leaves and woody ends. Cut into ½- to 1-inch pieces. Freeze for best quality.	Not recommended	In a saucepan sprinkle ½ cup sugar over each 4 cups fruit; mix well. Let stand until juice appears. Bring slowly to boiling, stirring gently. Fill jars with hot fruit and juice, leaving ½ inch headspace. Process pints and quarts for 15 minutes.	Blanch for 1 minute; cool quickly and drain. Use a syrup or unsweetened pack, leaving the recommended headspace. Or use a sugar pack of ½ cup sugar to each 3 cups fruit.

CANNING AND FREEZING TOMATOES

Allow 2½ to 3 pounds unblemished tomatoes per quart. Wash tomatoes. To peel, dip tomatoes in boiling water for 30 seconds or until skins start to split. Dip in cold water; skin and core. Continue as directed below.

TOMATOES	PREPARATION	BOILING-WATER CANNING	PRESSURE CANNING*	FREEZING
CRUSHED	Wash and peel tomatoes. Cut into quarters; add enough to a large pan to cover bottom. Crush with a wooden spoon. Heat and stir until boiling. Slowly add remaining pieces, stirring constantly. Simmer for 5 minutes. Fill jars. Add bottled lemon juice: 1 tablespoon for pints, 2 tablespoons for quarts. Add salt, if desired: ¼ to ½ teaspoon for pints, ½ to 1 teaspoon for quarts. Leave ½ inch headspace.	Process pints for 35 minutes and quarts for 45 minutes.	Process pints and quarts for 15 minutes.	Set pan of tomatoes in ice water to cool. Fill containers, leaving a 1-inch headspace.
WHOLE OR HALVED, NO ADDED LIQUID	Wash and peel tomatoes; halve, if desired. Fill jars, pressing to fill spaces with juice. Add bottled lemon juice: 1 tablespoon for pints, 2 tablespoons for quarts. Add salt, if desired: ¼ to ½ teaspoon for pints, ½ to 1 teaspoon for quarts. Leave a ½-inch headspace.	Process pints and quarts for 85 minutes.	Process pints and quarts for 25 minutes.	Fill freezer containers, leaving a 1-inch headspace. (Use only for cooking, due to texture changes caused by freezing.)
WHOLE OR HALVED, WATER-PACKED	Wash and peel tomatoes; halve, if desired. Fill jars. Add bottled lemon juice: 1 tablespoon for pints, 2 tablespoons for quarts. Add salt, if desired: ¼ to ½ teaspoon for pints, ½ to 1 teaspoon for quarts. Add boiling water, leaving a ½-inch headspace. Or heat tomatoes in saucepan with enough water to cover; simmer 5 minutes. Fill jars with tomatoes and cooking liquid. Add bottled lemon juice and salt (if desired) in the amounts listed above. Leave ½ inch headspace.	Process pints for 40 minutes and quarts for 45 minutes.	Process pints and quarts for 10 minutes.	If heated, set pan of tomatoes in cold water to cool. Fill containers, leaving a 1-inch headspace.

*For a dial-gauge canner, use 11 pounds of pressure; for a weighted-gauge canner, use 10 pounds of pressure. At altitudes above 1,000 feet, see tip, page 191.
NOTE: Add salt, if desired: ¼ to ½ teaspoon for pints and ½ to 1 teaspoon for quarts.

Chapter Two

FRUITS & VEGETABLES

Start with perfect produce, fresh from the garden and bursting with flavor. Then prepare it simply with little more than the slightest touch of salt or sugar. Or give it an interesting twist with a tangy brine or exotic spices. Savor the results for months to come.

CANNING FRUITS AND VEGETABLES

At the height of the season, when your garden or farmers' markets are overflowing, it's rewarding (and smart) to preserve the bounty. From the first strawberries of late spring to the last peppers right before frost, you'll find canning them satisfying and simple.

❶ FOOD MILL This handy utensil processes any food into a smooth puree, such as apples for apple butter or applesauce, or tomatoes for sauces and ketchup. Bonus: It sieves out seeds and skins that a food processor or blender doesn't. It has many other uses in the kitchen as well.

❷ APPLE PEELER AND CORER If you are processing a lot of apples, this old-time device is worth the small investment. It peels, cores, and slices an apple in seconds. Models differ slightly, with most using suction to firmly attach the base to a table or countertop.

❸ CHERRY PITTER This small handtool uses spring action to efficiently pop out the pit from each cherry one at a time. You can also use a small sharp knife or your fingers to pop out the pit.

  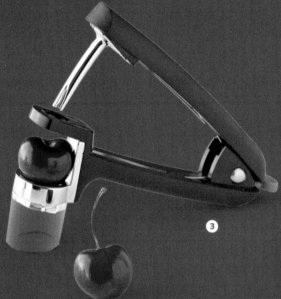

FRUITS AND VEGETABLES TROUBLESHOOTING

PROBLEM	CAUSE	SOLUTION
Fruit floats in the jar.	Fruit is lighter than the syrup or isn't packed in tightly.	Use firm, ripe fruit, which is heavier. Next time use a hot-pack method (see page 31), which makes fruit heavier as it absorbs more liquid. Use a light to medium syrup. Pack fruit as firmly as you can without crushing it.
Food at top of jar gets dark over time while in the jar.	The food came in contact with air.	Use a hot-pack method, which slightly breaks down food and ensures it will sink lower and pack better into the jar. Use a thin plastic spatula or other flexible, long tool around the sides when packing in food to remove air bubbles. Make sure food is completely covered with liquid when packing and always process for the recommended time in a current, reliable recipe.
Fruit gets darker after opening.	The food was not processed long enough or at a high enough temperature to inactivate enzymes.	Follow a current, reliable recipe. Start timing boiling-water canned goods only when water reaches a rolling boil, not before.
White sediment forms in the bottom of a jar of vegetables.	This could be simply starch from the food or minerals in the water used. However, if the liquid is murky or the food is soft, it could be bacterial spoilage. Do not eat.	There is no way to inactivate starches in foods. Mineral deposits from water can be avoided by using soft water. Bacterial spoilage occurs when food isn't processed correctly (review Chapter 1) or long enough.
Apples, pears, and peaches take on a purple to red color.	A natural chemical change has occurred during the heating process.	None. The change is harmless.
Black spots form on the underside of the metal lid.	Natural compounds in some foods make a brown or black deposit on the inside of the lid.	None. The deposits are harmless as long as there is no gray (which indicates mold) and there is no unpleasant or odd smell.

Preserve the best of summer in a jar. Choose fully ripe, unblemished tomatoes and allow 2½ to 3 pounds per quart.

HOME-CANNED TOMATOES

PREP: 30 MINUTES **PROCESS:** 85 MINUTES **MAKES:** 4 QUARTS OR 8 PINTS

2½ to 3 pounds tomatoes per quart; 1¼ to 1½ pounds tomatoes per pint

Bottled lemon juice

Salt

❶ Wash, core, and peel tomatoes. Keep whole, cut in half, or cut up, as desired. Pack tomatoes into hot, sterilized canning jars, leaving a ½-inch headspace. Add 1 tablespoon bottled lemon juice per pint or 2 tablespoons per quart. If desired, add ¼ to ½ teaspoon salt to each pint or ½ to 1 teaspoon to each quart.

❷ Wipe jar rims; adjust lids. Process pints and quarts in a boiling-water canner for 85 minutes (start timing when water returns to boil). Remove jars from canner; cool on wire racks.

CRUSHED TOMATOES: Cut washed, peeled tomatoes into quarters; add enough tomatoes to a large pot to cover bottom. Crush with a wooden spoon. Heat and stir until boiling. Slowly add remaining pieces, stirring constantly. Simmer for 5 minutes. Fill hot, sterilized canning jars with tomatoes, leaving a ½-inch headspace. Add lemon juice and salt as above. Wipe jar rims; adjust lids. Process filled jars in a boiling-water canner for 45 minutes for quarts or 35 minutes for pints (start timing when water returns to boil). Remove jars from canner; cool on wire racks.

PER ¼-CUP SERVING: 13 cal., 0 g total fat, 0 mg chol., 4 mg sodium, 3 g carbo., 1 g fiber, 1 g pro.

On its own in a tumbler or dressed up as a Bloody Mary in a fancy glass, Tomato Juice Cocktail is a delicious way to sip your veggies.

TOMATO JUICE COCKTAIL

PREP: 1 HOUR **COOK:** 45 MINUTES **PROCESS:** 35 MINUTES **MAKES:** ABOUT 4 PINTS (16 SERVINGS)

8   **pounds tomatoes**

1   **cup chopped celery (2 stalks)**

½   **cup chopped onion (1 medium)**

6   **tablespoons bottled lemon juice**

2   **tablespoons sugar**

1   **tablespoon Worcestershire sauce**

2   **teaspoons prepared horseradish**

1   **teaspoon salt**

¼   **teaspoon bottled hot pepper sauce**

1 Wash tomatoes. Remove stem ends and cores. Cut tomatoes into pieces; drain. Measure 19 cups cut-up tomatoes.

2 In an 8- or 10-quart heavy kettle or pot combine tomatoes, celery, and onion. Bring to boiling over low heat, stirring frequently. Simmer, covered, about 15 minutes or until tomatoes are soft, stirring frequently to prevent sticking.

3 Press tomato mixture through a food mill or sieve to extract juice; measure 12 cups juice. Discard solids. Return juice to kettle. Bring to boiling. Boil gently, uncovered, for 20 minutes, stirring often. Measure juice (you should have 9½ to 10 cups). Stir in lemon juice, sugar, Worcestershire sauce, horseradish, salt, and hot pepper sauce. Return to boiling; reduce heat. Simmer, uncovered, for 10 minutes more.

4 Immediately ladle hot juice into hot, sterilized pint canning jars, leaving a ½-inch headspace. Wipe jar rims; adjust lids. Process filled jars in a boiling-water canner for 35 minutes (start timing when water returns to boil). Remove jars from canner; cool on wire racks.

PER ½-CUP SERVING: 61 cal., 1 g total fat (0 g sat. fat), 0 mg chol., 181 mg sodium, 14 g carbo., 3 g fiber, 2 g pro.

Come September, when the garden is producing a little of this and a little of that, this tangy medley brings contrasting flavors, textures, and colors together into one remarkable side dish.

PICKLED GARDEN VEGETABLES

PREP: 90 MINUTES **PROCESS:** 5 MINUTES **MAKES:** 7 PINTS (56 SERVINGS)

1	**pound carrots**
1	**pound fresh green beans, trimmed and cut into 2-inch pieces**
3	**cups cauliflower florets**
3	**green and/or red sweet peppers, cut into strips**
2	**zucchini and/or yellow summer squash, halved lengthwise and cut into 1/2-inch slices, or 1 pound baby zucchini or yellow summer squash, halved**
2	**medium onions, cut into wedges**
3	**cups water**
3	**cups white wine vinegar**
2	**tablespoons sugar**
1	**tablespoon pickling salt**
3	**tablespoons snipped fresh dill**
1/2	**teaspoon crushed red pepper**
6	**cloves garlic, minced**

1 Halve any large carrots lengthwise. Using a crinkle cutter or sharp knife, cut carrots into 1/4-inch slices. In an 8-quart kettle combine carrots, green beans, cauliflower, sweet peppers, zucchini, and onions. Add enough water to cover. Bring to boiling. Cook, uncovered, for 3 minutes. Drain.

2 Pack vegetables into hot, sterilized pint canning jars, leaving a 1/2-inch headspace. Set aside.

3 In a large saucepan combine the 3 cups water, the vinegar, sugar, salt, dill, crushed red pepper, and garlic. Bring to boiling. Pour hot liquid over vegetables in jars, leaving 1/2 inch headspace. Wipe jar rims; adjust lids. Process filled jars in a boiling-water canner for 5 minutes (start timing when water returns to boil). Remove jars from canner; cool on wire racks.

PER 1/4-CUP SERVING: 14 cal., 0 g total fat, 0 mg chol., 71 mg sodium, 3 g carbo., 0 g fiber, 0 g pro.

For the best flavor, let these garlicky beans stand in a cool, dark place for 2 weeks before serving or sharing.

PICKLED DILLED GREEN BEANS

PREP: 45 MINUTES **COOK:** 5 MINUTES **PROCESS:** 5 MINUTES **MAKES:** 5 PINTS (ABOUT 20 SERVINGS)

3 pounds fresh green beans

5 fresh red serrano chile peppers (optional)

3 cups water

3 cups white wine vinegar

1 tablespoon pickling salt

1 tablespoon sugar

3 tablespoons snipped fresh dill or 1 tablespoon dried dill

1/2 teaspoon crushed red pepper

6 cloves garlic, minced

5 small heads fresh dill (optional)

❶ Wash beans; drain. If desired, trim ends. Place enough water to cover beans in an 8-quart kettle or pot. Bring to boiling. Add beans and, if desired, fresh chile peppers to the boiling water; return to boiling. Cook, uncovered, for 5 minutes. Drain.

❷ Pack hot beans lengthwise into hot, sterilized pint canning jars, cutting beans to fit if necessary and leaving a 1/2-inch headspace. Place one hot pepper (if using) into each jar so that it shows through the glass. Set aside.

❸ In a large saucepan combine the 3 cups water, vinegar, pickling salt, sugar, the 3 tablespoons fresh dill, crushed red pepper, and garlic. Bring to boiling. Pour over beans in jars, leaving a 1/2-inch headspace. If desired, add small heads of fresh dill to jars. Wipe jar rims; adjust lids. Process filled jars in a boiling-water canner for 5 minutes (start timing when water returns to boil). Remove jars from canner; cool on wire racks.

PER 1/2-CUP SERVING: 42 cal., 0 g total fat, 0 mg chol., 357 mg sodium, 7 g carbo., 3 g fiber, 2 g pro.

Although the recipe calls for small whole beets, you can use larger ones. Just remove the tops before cooking. After cooking and removing skin, cut them into 1-inch cubes or ¼-inch slices.

PICKLED BEETS

PREP: 15 MINUTES **COOK:** 30 MINUTES **PROCESS:** 30 MINUTES **MAKES:** 6 HALF-PINTS (21 SERVINGS)

3 pounds small whole beets (2-inch diameter)

2 cups vinegar

1 cup water

½ cup sugar

1 teaspoon whole allspice

6 whole cloves

3 inches stick cinnamon

❶ Wash beets, leaving roots and 1 inch of tops intact. Place beets in a 4- to 6-quart kettle or pot; add enough water to cover. Bring to boiling; reduce heat. Simmer, uncovered, about 25 minutes or until tender; drain. Cool beets slightly; trim off roots and stems. Slip off the skins.

❷ Empty the kettle of the water, which may be slightly gritty or dirty. Rinse, wash, and dry the kettle. In the clean kettle combine vinegar, water, and sugar. Make a spice bag by placing allspice, cloves, and cinnamon on a double-thick, 7-inch square of 100-percent-cotton cheesecloth. Bring corners together and tie with clean kitchen string. Add spice bag to kettle. Heat to boiling; reduce heat. Simmer, uncovered, for 5 minutes. Discard the spice bag.

❸ Pack beets in hot, sterilized half-pint canning jars, leaving a ½-inch headspace. Carefully add the boiling pickling liquid, leaving a ½-inch headspace. Wipe jar rims; adjust lids. Process filled jars in a boiling-water canner for 30 minutes (start timing when water returns to boil). Remove jars from canner; cool on wire racks.

PER ⅓-CUP SERVING: 29 cal., 0 g total fat, 0 mg chol., 17 mg sodium, 8 g carbo., 1 g fiber, 0 g pro.

Enjoy cocktail onions as part of a relish tray or in a Gibson cocktail—that's a martini garnished with a cocktail onion instead of an olive.

COCKTAIL ONIONS

PREP: 1 HOUR **PROCESS:** 10 MINUTES **MAKES:** 6 HALF-PINTS (24 SERVINGS)

2	quarts pearl onions (about 2 1/4 pounds)
6	small hot chile peppers (fresh or dried)*
6	bay leaves
6	thin slices fresh horseradish root
1 1/2	teaspoons mustard seed
1	cup white vinegar
1	cup sherry vinegar or white wine vinegar
1/2	cup sugar
1/4	cup pickling salt

1 Blanch onions in boiling water for 3 minutes. Immediately transfer to a bowl of ice water to stop cooking. Peel onions. Place onions in hot, sterilized half-pint canning jars. To each jar add a chile pepper, bay leaf, horseradish slice, and 1/4 teaspoon mustard seed.

2 In a medium saucepan bring white vinegar, sherry vinegar, sugar, and pickling salt to boiling, stirring to dissolve sugar and salt.

3 Add liquid to canning jars, leaving a 1/4-inch headspace. Remove air bubbles. Wipe jar rims; adjust lids. Process in a boiling-water canner for 10 minutes (start timing when water returns to boil). Remove jars and cool on wire racks.

*NOTE: Try fresh Thai or bird peppers, or dried pequin, japones, or chile de arbol.

PER 3- TO 4-ONION SERVING: 39 cal., 0 g total fat, 0 mg chol., 970 mg sodium, 8 g carbo., 1 g fiber, 0 g pro.

An underappreciated vegetable, the humble cabbage is transformed by this pickling treatment into an aromatic, delicious, and beautifully hued condiment or side dish.

PICKLED RED CABBAGE

PREP: 1 1/2 HOURS **COOK:** 15 MINUTES **PROCESS:** 15 MINUTES **MAKES:** 5 PINTS (30 SERVINGS)

8	cups cider vinegar
3/4	cup packed brown sugar
1/2	cup water
1/4	cup pickling salt
1	teaspoon celery seeds
1	teaspoon cracked black pepper
1/2	teaspoon ground mace
1/2	teaspoon ground allspice
1/2	teaspoon ground cinnamon
4 1/2	pounds shredded red cabbage (28 cups)
1	medium red onion, halved and thinly sliced

❶ In an 8-quart Dutch oven bring vinegar, brown sugar, water, salt, celery seeds, pepper, mace, allspice, and cinnamon to boiling, stirring to dissolve sugar and salt. Gradually add cabbage and onion and return to boiling. Reduce heat and simmer, uncovered, for 15 minutes. Drain; reserving cooking liquid.

❷ Pack cabbage mixture into hot, sterilized 1-pint canning jars, leaving a 1-inch headspace. Ladle hot reserved liquid into jars, leaving a 1/4-inch headspace. Wipe jar rims; adjust lids. Process in a boiling-water canner for 15 minutes (start timing when water returns to boil). Remove jars and cool on racks.

PER 1/4-CUP SERVING: 53 cal., 0 g total fat, 0 mg chol., 791 mg sodium, 11 g carbo., 1 g fiber, 1 g pro.

Cauliflower is a favorite Indian vegetable. This recipe pays homage to its popularity with an exotic combination that includes hot peppers, ginger, turmeric, and mustard seed.

INDIAN CAULIFLOWER

PREP: 1 HOUR **PROCESS:** 15 MINUTES **MAKES:** 7 PINTS (42 SERVINGS)

- 2 **medium heads cauliflower**
- 1 **medium carrot, thinly bias-sliced**
- 1 **medium onion, cut in thin wedges**
- 2 **fresh serrano peppers, sliced***
- 2 **tablespoons olive oil**
- 8 **cloves garlic, sliced**
- 1 **tablespoon grated fresh ginger**
- 2 **teaspoons ground turmeric**
- 2 **teaspoons cumin seeds**
- 1 **teaspoon mustard seeds**
- 4 ½ **cups white vinegar**
- 4 ½ **cups water**
- 4 **teaspoons pickling salt**

1 Chop enough cauliflower to equal 12 cups florets. In a very large bowl combine cauliflower, carrot, onion, serrano peppers, olive oil, garlic, ginger, turmeric, cumin seeds, and mustard seeds. Toss well to combine. Pack mixture into hot, sterilized pint-size canning jars.

2 In a Dutch oven bring vinegar, water, and salt to boiling. Ladle liquid into canning jars, leaving a ½-inch headspace. Wipe jar rims, adjust lids. Process in a boiling-water canner for 15 minutes (start timing when water returns to boil). Remove jars and cool on racks.

*NOTE: Because hot chile peppers, such as serranos, contain volatile oils that can burn skin and eyes, avoid direct contact with chiles as much as possible. When working with chile peppers, wear plastic or rubber gloves. If bare hands do touch the chile pepper, wash well with soap and water.

PER ¼-CUP SERVING: 21 cal., 1 g total fat (0 g sat. fat), 0 mg chol., 194 mg sodium, 2 g carbo., 1 g fiber, 1 g pro.

For best results, use those apples deemed best for cooking, such as Jonathans, McIntosh, and Rome Beauty. They have a complex flavor and softer texture that make for an excellent sauce.

APPLESAUCE

PREP: 1 HOUR **COOK:** 25 MINUTES **PROCESS:** 15 MINUTES FOR PINTS, 25 MINUTES FOR QUARTS **MAKES:** ABOUT 6 PINTS

8   pounds tart cooking apples, cored and quartered (24 cups)

2   cups water

¼   cup fresh lemon juice, strained

¾   to 1¼ cups sugar

1 In an 8- to 10-quart heavy kettle or pot combine apples, water, and lemon juice. Bring to boiling; reduce heat. Simmer, covered, for 25 to 30 minutes until apples are very tender, stirring often.

2 Press apples through a food mill or sieve. Return pulp to kettle. Stir in sugar to taste. If necessary, add ½ to 1 cup water to reach desired consistency. Bring to boiling.

3 Ladle hot applesauce into hot, sterilized pint or quart canning jars, leaving a ½-inch headspace. Wipe jar rims; adjust lids. Process in a boiling-water canner for 15 minutes for pints or 20 minutes for quarts (start timing when water returns to a boil). Remove jars from canner; cool on wire racks.

RICH AND SPICY APPLESAUCE: Prepare as directed above, except add 10 inches stick cinnamon and 1½ teaspoons apple pie spice in Step 1. Simmer as directed. Remove stick cinnamon and discard. Substitute ¾ cup packed brown sugar for the granulated sugar. Stir in enough additional brown sugar to taste (¼ to ¾ cup).

VERY BERRY APPLESAUCE: Prepare as directed above, except replace 1 pound (4 cups) of the apples with 1 pound (4 cups) fresh or frozen thawed raspberries and/or strawberries and decrease water to 1½ cups in Step 1. Continue as directed above.

PER ½-CUP SERVING: 81 cal., 0 g total fat , 0 mg chol., 1 mg sodium, 21 g carbo., 2 g fiber, 0 g pro.

To make rings, use apples with a diameter of no more than 2½ inches. Preserve them in wide-mouth canning jars. If you use larger apples, cut each into eight wedges.

SPICED APPLE RINGS

PREP: 45 MINUTES **COOK:** 15 MINUTES **PROCESS:** 10 MINUTES **MAKES:** 7 PINTS (56 SERVINGS)

8   pounds firm tart apples
    Ascorbic acid color keeper*
10 3-inch pieces stick cinnamon
2   tablespoons whole cloves
1   1½-inch piece fresh ginger, sliced (optional)
6   cups packed brown sugar
6   cups water
1   cup cider vinegar

❶ Wash, peel, and core 1 apple; cut crosswise into ½-inch rings. Place apple rings in ascorbic acid color-keeper solution as soon as peeled and cut. Repeat with remaining apples.

❷ Make a spice bag by placing cinnamon pieces, whole cloves, and, if desired, ginger on a double-thick 7-inch square cheesecloth. Bring corners together and tie with clean kitchen string. Set spice bag aside.

❸ In an 8-quart kettle or pot combine brown sugar, water, and vinegar. Heat to boiling, stirring constantly. Reduce heat; add spice bag. Simmer, covered, for 10 minutes.

❹ Drain apple slices; add to hot liquid. Return to boiling; reduce heat. Simmer, covered, about 5 minutes or until apples are tender, stirring occasionally. Discard spice bag. Using a slotted spoon, pack apple rings into clean, hot, sterilized canning jars, leaving a ½-inch headspace. Add hot liquid, leaving a ½-inch headspace. Wipe jar rims; adjust lids. Process filled jars in a boiling-water canner for 10 minutes (start timing when water returns to boil). Remove jars from canner; cool on wire racks.

*NOTE: To prevent fruits such as apples and pears from darkening when peeled or cut and exposed to air, treat the fruit with ascorbic acid color keeper. Look for it in the produce section or with canning supplies in the supermarket. To use ascorbic acid color keeper, follow package directions.

PER ¼-CUP SERVING: 103 cal., 0 g total fat, 0 mg chol., 7 mg sodium, 27 g carbo., 1 g fiber, 0 g pro.

For the best flavor, choose ripe pears for this mint-infused recipe. If the pears are too firm, place them in a paper bag and allow them to stand at room temperature for a few days. When ripe, they'll yield to gentle pressure. These are delicious served with a spoonful of crème fraîche.

MINTED PEARS

PREP: 35 MINUTES **COOK:** 10 MINUTES **PROCESS:** 20 MINUTES FOR PINTS, 25 MINUTES FOR QUARTS
MAKES: 7 PINTS (20 SERVINGS)

1 **cup lightly packed mint leaves**

1 **cup water**

5 $\frac{2}{3}$ **cups water**

$\frac{3}{4}$ **cup sugar**

7 **pounds pears (about 20)**

Ascorbic acid color keeper (see Note, page 68)

❶ In a small saucepan mash the mint leaves with the back of a spoon. Stir in the 1 cup water; heat to boiling. Remove from heat; let stand for 10 minutes. Strain liquid through a fine-mesh sieve, pressing on leaves with the back of a spoon; discard leaves. Set mint-flavored water aside.

❷ For syrup, in a 4- to 6-quart kettle or pot combine the 5⅔ cups water and sugar. Heat until sugar dissolves. Add the mint-flavored water. Keep syrup hot, but do not boil.

❸ Wash, peel, halve, and core pears; place pear halves in ascorbic acid color-keeper solution as soon as peeled and cut. Drain pear halves; add to syrup. Heat to boiling. Boil, covered, for 5 minutes.

❹ Using a slotted spoon, pack hot pear halves into hot, sterilized pint or quart canning jars, leaving a ½-inch headspace. Cover with the hot syrup, leaving a ½-inch headspace. Wipe jar rims; adjust lids. Process filled jars in a boiling-water canner for 20 minutes for pints or 25 minutes for quarts (start timing when water returns to boil). Remove jars from canner; cool on wire racks.

PER 2 PEAR HALVES: 163 cal., 1 g total fat (0 g sat. fat), 0 mg chol., 3 mg sodium, 42 g carbo., 4 g fiber, 1 g pro.

Brandy and ginger infuse these pears with an intense flavor that makes them a great gift—or a great dessert—for the holidays.

BRANDIED HONEY-AND-SPICE PEARS

PREP: 35 MINUTES **PROCESS:** 20 MINUTES **MAKES:** 6 PINTS (15 SERVINGS)

6	**pounds pears (about 15 pears)**
	Ascorbic acid color-keeper (see Note, page 68)
4	**cups cranberry juice, apple juice, or apple cider**
1½	**cups honey**
½	**cup lemon juice**
3	**tablespoons chopped candied ginger**
8	**inches stick cinnamon, broken into 2-inch pieces**
½	**teaspoon whole cloves**
¼	**cup brandy**

❶ Wash, peel, halve, and core pears; place pear halves in ascorbic acid color-keeper solution as soon as peeled and cut.

❷ For syrup, in a 6- to 8-quart kettle or pot combine cranberry juice, honey, lemon juice, candied ginger, stick cinnamon, and whole cloves. Heat to boiling. Drain pear halves. Add pear halves and brandy to syrup. Return to boiling; reduce heat. Simmer, uncovered, about 5 minutes or until pears are almost tender, stirring occasionally.

❸ Pack hot pears into hot, sterilized pint canning jars, leaving a ½-inch headspace. Cover with hot syrup, leaving a ½-inch headspace. Wipe jar rims; adjust lids. Process in a boiling-water canner for 20 minutes (start timing when water returns to boil). Remove jars from canner; cool on wire racks.

PER 2 PEAR HALVES: 261 cal., 0 g total fat, 0 mg chol., 5 mg sodium, 67 g carbo., 6 g fiber, 1 g pro.

Dark sweet cherries add a rosy tint to this refreshing blend of pineapple, pears, and peaches.

ROSY FRUIT COCKTAIL

PREP: 1 HOUR **PROCESS:** 20 MINUTES **MAKES:** 9 PINTS (36 SERVINGS)

5 ¼ cups Light Syrup
1 2-pound pineapple
3 pounds peaches
3 pounds pears
1 pound dark sweet cherries
1 pound seedless green grapes

❶ Prepare Light Syrup; keep hot but not boiling.

❷ Wash fruit. Using a large sharp knife, slice off the bottom stem end and the green top of pineapple. Stand pineapple upright and slice off the skin in wide strips from top to bottom; discard skin. To remove the eyes, cut diagonally around the fruit, following the pattern of the eyes and making narrow wedge-shape grooves into the pineapple. Cut away as little of the meat as possible. Cut pineapple in half lengthwise; place pieces cut sides down and cut lengthwise again. Cut off and discard center core from each quarter. Cut pineapple into chunks. Measure 3 cups pineapple. Peel, pit, and cut peaches into chunks. Measure 8½ cups peaches. Peel, core, and cut pears into chunks. Measure 6½ cups pears. Place pear chunks in ascorbic acid color-keeper solution as soon as peeled and cut. Halve and pit cherries. Measure 2½ cups cherries. Remove stems from grapes. Measure 3 cups grapes.

❸ In a 4- or 6-quart kettle or pot combine pineapple, peaches, drained pears, cherries, and grapes. Add hot syrup; heat to boiling.

❹ Pack hot fruit and syrup in hot, sterilized jars, leaving a ½-inch headspace. Wipe jar rims; adjust lids. Process filled jars in a boiling-water canner for 20 minutes for half-pints or pints (start timing when water returns to boil). Remove jars from canner; cool on wire racks.

LIGHT SYRUP: In a large saucepan cook and stir 1¼ cups sugar and 5 cups water over medium heat until sugar dissolves. Makes 5¾ cups. (Use any remaining syrup to sweeten iced tea or use in cocktails.)

PER ½-CUP SERVING WITH LIGHT SYRUP: 108 cal., 0 g total fat, 0 mg chol., 1 mg sodium, 27 g carbo., 2 g fiber, 1 g pro.

Make a pie in a flash using local apples that you've canned yourself. This filling makes a pie with softer fruit than fresh but with the same great flavor.

APPLE PIE FILLING

PREP: 75 MINUTES PROCESS: 25 MINUTES MAKES: 7 QUARTS (ENOUGH FOR 7 PIES)

1	lemon
10	to 12 pounds cooking apples (about 24), peeled
5 ½	cups sugar
1 ½	cups ClearJel*
1	tablespoon ground cinnamon
½	teaspoon ground nutmeg
⅛	teaspoon ground cloves
5	cups apple juice
2 ½	cups cold water
¾	cup bottled lemon juice

❶ Fill 2 large bowls half full with cold water. Squeeze 1 lemon half into water in each bowl. Using an apple slicer, core and cut apples into wedges (or slice by hand into ½- to ¾-inch wedges). As you slice the apples, place slices in the water mixture in bowls to keep them from browning.

❷ In a 6- to 8-quart pot bring water to boiling. Drain apples; measure 24 cups. Add 6 cups apples at a time to the boiling water. Cook 30 seconds per batch. Use a large slotted spoon to remove apples from boiling water to a large bowl. Cover bowl to keep apples hot.

❸ In the 6- to 8-quart pot combine sugar, ClearJel, cinnamon, nutmeg, and cloves. Stir in apple juice and the 2½ cups cold water. Cook over medium-high heat, stirring constantly, until mixture thickens and boils. Add ¾ cup lemon juice; boil for 1 minute, stirring constantly. Stir in apples (mixture will be thick).

❹ Pack hot apple mixture into hot, sterilized quart canning jars, leaving a 1-inch headspace. Wipe rims; adjust lids. Process in a boiling-water canner for 25 minutes (start timing when water returns to boil). Remove jars from canner; cool on wire racks.

*NOTE: ClearJel is a food starch used for thickening in canning. Unlike regular cornstarch, ClearJel doesn't break down under intense heat nor after reheating.

PER ½ CUP FILLING: 175 cal., 0 g total fat, 0 mg chol., 2 mg sodium, 45 g carbo., 1 g fiber, 0 g pro.

Get together a group and go berrying! Plan to use the fresh blueberries within a day or two of picking or purchasing. Turn them into this rich-tasting filling that will make fantastic pies during the winter and early spring.

BLUEBERRY PIE FILLING

PREP: 30 MINUTES **PROCESS:** 30 MINUTES **MAKES:** 7 QUARTS (ENOUGH FOR 7 PIES)

3 quarts water
8 quarts fresh blueberries
8 cups sugar
3 cups ClearJel
   (see Note, page 76)
9 cups cold water
$2/3$ cup bottled lemon juice

1 Rinse and drain blueberries. In a 6- to 8-quart kettle or pot heat the 3 quarts water to boiling. Add 8 cups of the blueberries; return to boiling. Using a slotted spoon, transfer berries to a very large bowl. Repeat with remaining berries, adding berries in 8-cup portions and returning water to boiling with each addition.

2 In a large saucepan combine sugar and ClearJel. Stir in the 9 cups cold water. Bring to boiling over medium-high heat, stirring constantly. Add lemon juice; boil for 1 minute, stirring constantly. Immediately pour over blueberries, stirring to coat.

3 Pack hot blueberry mixture into hot, sterilized quart canning jars, leaving a 1-inch headspace. Wipe jar rims; adjust lids. Process filled jars in a boiling-water canner for 30 minutes (start timing when water returns to boil). Remove jars from canner; cool on wire racks.

PER ½ CUP FILLING: 184 cal., 0 g total fat, 0 mg chol., 8 mg sodium, 47 g carbo., 2 g fiber, 1 g pro.

Hot-packing cherries usually results in better texture and flavor than cold-packing, but cold-packing is the easier method.

HOME-CANNED CHERRIES

PREP: 1 HOUR **PROCESS:** 20 MINUTES FOR QUARTS, 15 MINUTES FOR PINTS **MAKES:** YIELD VARIES

2 to 3 pounds fresh cherries per quart or 1 to 1 ½ pounds per pint

Ascorbic acid color keeper (see Note, page 68)

½ to ⅔ cup Light Syrup for each 2 cups fruit

HOT-PACK METHOD

❶ If desired, pit cherries, using a cherry pitter or a knife. If leaving unpitted, prick skin on opposite sides to prevent splitting. If desired, put cherries in ascorbic acid color-keeper solution to prevent browning; drain.

❷ In a kettle or pot combine cherries and hot Light Syrup. Bring to boiling. Remove from heat.

❸ Pack hot, sterilized canning jars with cherries and syrup, leaving a ½-inch headspace. Wipe jar rims; adjust lids. Process filled jars in boiling-water canner for 20 minutes for quarts or 15 minutes for pints (start timing when water returns to boil). Remove jars from canner; cool on wire racks.

LIGHT SYRUP: In a large saucepan combine 4 cups water and 1⅔ cups sugar. Heat until the sugar dissolves. Skim off foam as necessary. Use hot. Makes 4¼ cups.

RAW-PACK CHERRIES IN LIGHT SYRUP OR WATER: Pit or prick and treat cherries as directed in Step 1 above. Pack cherries in hot, sterilized canning jars, shaking gently to settle fruit, leaving a ½-inch headspace. Add boiling Light Syrup or water, leaving a ½-inch headspace. Wipe jar rims; adjust lids. Process filled jars in a boiling-water canner for 25 minutes for both quarts and pints (start timing when water returns to boil). Remove jars from canner; cool on wire racks.

PER ¼-CUP SERVING: 60 cal., 0 g total fat, 0 mg chol., 0 mg sodium, 15 g carbo., 1 g fiber, 1 g pro.

Choose peaches that are perfectly ripe but not mushy. Avoid peaches with large bruises—although small bruises and imperfections can be cut out with a knife.

HOME-CANNED PEACHES

PREP: 45 MINUTES **PROCESS:** 25 MINUTES FOR QUARTS, 20 MINUTES FOR PINTS **MAKES:** YIELD VARIES

2 **to 3 pounds fresh peaches per quart or 1 to 1½ pounds per pint**

Ascorbic acid color keeper (see Note, page 68)

½ **to ⅔ cup Light Syrup for each 2 cups fruit**

❶ Peel peaches by immersing in boiling water for 30 to 60 seconds or until skins start to split; remove and plunge into cold water. Remove skins from peaches. Halve and pit or slice. Treat with ascorbic acid color-keeper solution to prevent browning; drain.

❷ In a heavy kettle or pot combine peaches and hot Light Syrup. Bring to boiling. Fill hot, sterilized canning jars with fruit, placing halved fruits cut sides down. Top with additional syrup, leaving a ½-inch headspace.

❸ Wipe jar rims; adjust lids. Process filled jars in boiling-water canner for 25 minutes for quarts or 20 minutes for pints (start timing when water returns to boil). Remove jars from canner; cool on wire racks. (Note: For different syrup and packing options and information on packing in water, see page 31.)

LIGHT SYRUP: In a large saucepan combine 4 cups water and 1⅔ cups sugar. Stir and heat until the sugar dissolves. Skim off foam as necessary. Use hot. Makes 4¼ cups.

PER ¼-CUP SERVING: 40 cal., 0 g total fat, 0 mg chol., 0 mg sodium, 10 g carbo., 1 g fiber, 0 g pro.

If you're lucky enough to have a grape vine or two, you know that it's a challenge to process the abundance of fruit. Homemade grape juice is a refreshing way to take all those grapes and cook them down to their flavorful essence.

GRAPE JUICE

PREP: 45 MINUTES **PROCESS:** 5 MINUTES **STAND:** 24 HOURS **MAKES:** ABOUT 2 QUARTS (8 SERVINGS)

7   to 8 pounds
    Concord grapes
½   to 1 cup sugar (optional)

❶ Wash grapes; remove from stems. Measure 17 cups grapes. In a 6-quart kettle or pot combine grapes and 2½ cups water; cover. Bring just to a simmer. Cover; simmer for 10 to 15 minutes or until grapes are softened, occasionally stirring gently.

❷ Remove from heat; strain through a canning jelly bag or colander lined with several layers of cheesecloth, pressing on grapes gently to extract juice. Transfer juice to a large clean pitcher. Cover; refrigerate for 24 hours. Without stirring, pour off and reserve clear liquid; discard sediment that collects at the bottom of the pitcher. If desired, for clearer juice, pour juice through a sieve lined with a coffee filter.

❸ In a large pot or kettle combine grape juice and, if using, sugar. Heat just to simmering, stirring to dissolve sugar.

❹ Skim any foam that collects on surface of juice. Ladle hot juice into clean, hot quart canning jars, leaving a ¼-inch headspace. Wipe jar rims; adjust lids. Process in a boiling-water canner for 5 minutes (start timing when water returns to boil). Remove jars from canner; cool on wire racks. Chill thoroughly before serving.

PER 8-OUNCE SERVING: 154 cal., 1 g total fat (0 g sat. fat), 0 mg chol., 5 mg sodium, 39 g carbo., 2 g fiber, 1 g pro.

Chapter Three

PICKLES

Pack a peck of perfect pickles into a jar! From classic dills to unusual pickled vegetables—and even watermelon rind—you'll find a world of flavor in produce preserved in a tangy, salty brine.

MAKING PICKLES

Sure, you can buy pickles at the supermarket, but homemade pickles are a special treat. Try traditional favorites or experiment with interesting new combinations that go beyond cucumbers, incorporating green tomatoes, watermelon, sweet onions, cauliflower, and more.

Decades ago pickle making was a serious business. Large crocks holding gallons of cucumbers, cabbage, and other vegetables filled kitchens. Housewives carefully watched and skimmed brine as the pickles underwent a lengthy fermentation process.

These days you can make tasty pickles in a day rather than a month. There are even mixes for instant brines and some methods that skip heat processing altogether. A wide variety of recipes means you can pickle almost any type of fruit or vegetable.

WHICH CUCUMBERS TO USE?

Not all types of cucumbers work well for making pickles.

The best cucumbers to use are pickling cucumbers, sometimes called Kirby cucumbers. They are small—just a few to several inches long—making them easier to pack into a jar. Also they have firm flesh with fewer seeds and their skins are thinner to better allow brine to penetrate.

Regular, larger garden cucumbers can be used, but they don't work as well. You also can use supermarket English cucumbers, which are long, slender, and wrapped in plastic (though they are prohibitively expensive for large canning projects).

What you shouldn't use is the common waxed cucumber sold at supermarkets. The waxy coating keeps the cucumber fresher longer, but it interferes with the cucumber's ability to absorb brine. Test for waxy coating by scraping your thumbnail along the cucumber.

TYPES OF PICKLES

FERMENTED PICKLES Sometimes also called brined pickles, these are submerged in a salty solution to ferment or cure up to 6 weeks, either at room temperature or in the refrigerator.

HOT-PACK PICKLES Cucumbers are simmered in brine and packed, still hot, into hot, sterilized jars. Part of the process often includes marinating the cucumbers in the brine for several hours or a day or two before canning. They're then reheated before packing into jars and processing. Hot-pack pickles are less likely to float and less likely to spoil because air is removed as they simmer.

FRESH-PACK PICKLES Also called raw-pack or cold-pack, this method is putting cucumbers directly in the jar—fresh—and topping with hot brine before processing.

REFRIGERATOR PICKLES Also called "easy" pickles, in this method cucumbers are combined with a brine, packed into containers, and stored in the refrigerator for up to several weeks.

PICKLED VEGETABLES Other vegetables are popular for pickling, including cabbage (sometimes made into sauerkraut or kim chee), onions, beets, cauliflower, peppers, and carrots. The packing process can be fermented, hot-pack, fresh-pack, or refrigerator brining.

PICKLED FRUITS Fruit is simmered in a spicy, sweet, or sour syrup, or brine and then processed. Cherries and watermelon rinds are two of the most commonly pickled fruits. These, too, can use a variety of methods for processing.

PREPARING CUCUMBERS The blossom end of a cucumber (the end opposite the stem) has a concentration of enzymes. These enzymes hasten the decomposition of foods, so slice off the blossom end before processing to minimize enzymes in pickles.

PICKLES TROUBLESHOOTING

PROBLEM	CAUSE	SOLUTION
Soft or slippery pickles.	Enzymes, which soften pickles, were not inactivated or the brine and heat didn't work in preserving the pickles properly.	Always cut off the blossom end of the cucumbers because enzymes are concentrated there. Make sure the brine is full-strength (measure carefully) and use pure, refined, or pickling salt. Remove scum daily during a long brining process. Cover pickles completely with liquid during any fermentation times and when processing in jars. Process all pickles in boiling-water canner, not a pressure canner.
Pickles shrivel in the jar.	Cucumbers did not properly absorb brine.	Precisely measure salt, sugar, and vinegar and mix well before adding to cucumbers. Prick whole cucumbers before canning. Never use waxed cucumbers (you can tell by scraping your nail along the peel).
Pickles darken or discolor in the jar	Minerals or metals reacted with the brine, or spices were too fine or left in.	Use soft water when making brine. Use nonmetallic, nonreactive pans, bowls, and utensils when making pickles. Use whole spices, rather than ground, and remove them as the recipe directs.
White sediment forms in the bottom of pickle jar.	Yeasts have developed on the surface and settled or additives in salt have settled. (If there is any sign of spoilage or an odd smell, discard.)	The yeasts are harmless, as is the sediment if the amount of sediment is small. Use canning or pickling salt, which is specially formulated to be free of additives that can cloud or mar brine.

Classic dill pickles are so mouthwatering you can enjoy them all on their own. Also try them neatly sliced on sandwiches, as a multipurpose relish, or a sweet and spicy variation.

DILL PICKLES

PREP: 30 MINUTES **PROCESS:** 10 MINUTES **STAND:** 1 WEEK **MAKES:** 6 PINTS (36 PICKLES)

3 pounds 4-inch pickling cucumbers (about 36) (see page 88)

3 cups water

3 cups white vinegar

¼ cup pickling salt

¼ cup sugar

6 to 9 heads fresh dill or 6 tablespoons dill seeds

❶ Thoroughly rinse cucumbers. Remove stems and cut off a slice from each blossom end. In a large stainless steel, enameled, or nonstick saucepan combine water, vinegar, pickling salt, and sugar. Bring to boiling.

❷ Pack cucumbers loosely into hot, sterilized pint canning jars, leaving a ½-inch headspace. Add 2 to 3 heads of dill or 1 tablespoon dill seeds to each jar. Pour hot vinegar mixture over cucumbers, leaving a ½-inch headspace. Discard any remaining hot vinegar mixture. Wipe jar rims; adjust lids. Process in a boiling-water canner for 10 minutes (begin timing when water returns to boiling). Remove jars; cool on racks. Store. Let stand for 1 week to develop flavors before serving.

PER PICKLE: 10 cal., 0 g total fat, 0 mg chol., 389 mg sodium, 2 g carbo., 0 g fiber, 0 g pro.

HAMBURGER DILL PICKLES: Prepare as above, except cut pickles into ¼-inch slices.

SWEET AND SPICY DILL PICKLES: Prepare as above, except substitute cider vinegar for white vinegar and add 2 hot red chile peppers, seeded and minced, to vinegar mixture. When adding dill to each jar, also add to each jar ½ tablespoon mustard seeds, 1 bay leaf, ½ tablespoon black peppercorns, and 1 clove garlic, halved. (Shown, *opposite.*)

DILL PICKLE RELISH: Prepare as above, except seed and finely chop enough cucumbers to equal 8 cups. Reduce water to 1½ cups and vinegar to 1½ cups. Use a 4- to 5-quart pot. Stir cucumbers into boiling vinegar mixture with 3 tablespoons dill seeds. Return to boiling. Cook, uncovered, for 5 minutes. Ladle into hot, sterilized pint canning jars, leaving a ½-inch headspace. Wipe jar rims; adjust lids. Process as above. Makes 4 pints.

Few things are as satisfying as putting up homemade pickles from a bumper crop of summer cucumbers. These sweet and crisp pickles make an old-fashioned complement to meals all year.

BREAD-AND-BUTTER PICKLES

PREP: 50 MINUTES **COOK:** 25 MINUTES **PROCESS:** 10 MINUTES
CHILL: 3 TO 12 HOURS **MAKES:** 7 PINTS (70 SERVINGS)

4	**quarts sliced medium cucumbers (see page 88)**
8	**medium white onions, sliced**
⅓	**cup pickling salt**
3	**cloves garlic, halved**
	Cracked ice
4	**cups sugar**
3	**cups cider vinegar**
2	**tablespoons mustard seeds**
1½	**teaspoons turmeric**
1½	**teaspoons celery seeds**

❶ In a 6- to 8-quart stainless-steel, enamel, or nonstick kettle or pot combine cucumber slices, onions, pickling salt, and garlic. Add 2 inches of cracked ice. Cover with lid and refrigerate for 3 to 12 hours.

❷ Remove any remaining ice. Drain mixture well in a large colander. Remove garlic.

❸ In the same kettle combine sugar, vinegar, mustard seeds, turmeric, and celery seeds. Heat to boiling. Add cucumber mixture. Return to boiling.

❹ Pack hot cucumber mixture and liquid into hot, sterilized pint canning jars, leaving a ½-inch headspace. Wipe jar rims; adjust lids. Process in a boiling-water canner for 10 minutes (start timing when water returns to boil). Remove jars; cool on racks.

PER ¼-CUP SERVING: 33 cal., 0 g total fat, 0 mg chol., 266 mg sodium, 9 g carbo., 0 g fiber, 0 g pro.

Jalapeño peppers add kick to this tomato condiment. If you prefer a mild version, simply omit the hot peppers. If you crave more heat, substitute a hotter pepper, such as a serrano.

HOT PICKLED GREEN TOMATOES

PREP: 1 HOUR **PROCESS:** 15 MINUTES **MAKES:** 6 PINTS (42 SERVINGS)

3	pounds green tomatoes
3	medium onions, sliced
1	small red sweet pepper, chopped
¼	cup seeded and finely chopped jalapeño pepper*
4 ½	cups white vinegar
3	cups sugar
2	tablespoons mustard seeds
5	teaspoons whole peppercorns
2	teaspoons celery seeds

① Wash tomatoes. Remove cores; cut into ¼-inch slices. Measure 12 cups tomato slices. Combine tomato, onions, sweet pepper, and jalapeño pepper; set aside.

② In a large stainless-steel, enamel, or nonstick saucepan combine vinegar, sugar, mustard seeds, peppercorns, and celery seeds; heat to boiling.

③ Meanwhile, pack tomato mixture into hot, sterilized pint canning jars, leaving a ½-inch headspace. Pour hot vinegar mixture over vegetables, leaving a ½-inch headspace. Wipe jar rims; adjust lids. Process in a boiling-water canner for 15 minutes (start timing when water returns to boil). Remove jars from canner; cool on wire racks.

*NOTE: Because chile peppers, such as jalapeños contain volatile oils that can burn skin and eyes, avoid direct contact with them as much as possible. When working with chile peppers, wear plastic or rubber gloves. If your bare hands do touch the chile peppers, wash your hands well with soap and water.

PER ¼-CUP SERVING: 71 cal., 0 g total fat, 0 mg chol., 5 mg sodium, 19 g carbo., 0 g fiber, 1 g pro.

As Southern as fried chicken and pecan pie, these unusual pickles make thrifty and delicious use of what is usually tossed aside—the firm rind of a juicy watermelon.

WATERMELON RIND PICKLES

PREP: 1 HOUR **STAND:** OVERNIGHT **COOK:** 45 MINUTES **PROCESS:** 10 MINUTES
MAKES: 6 HALF-PINTS (24 SERVINGS)

1	**10-pound watermelon**
6	**cups water**
⅓	**cup pickling salt**
3½	**cups sugar**
1½	**cups white vinegar**
1½	**cups water**
15	**inches stick cinnamon, broken**
2	**teaspoons whole cloves**

1 Cut rind from watermelon (should have about 4½ pounds rind). Cut the green peel and pink flesh from the watermelon rind (the white portion); discard peel. Cut the rind into 1-inch squares. Measure 9 cups; place in a large bowl. Combine the 6 cups water and pickling salt; pour over rind (add more water if necessary to cover). Cover and let stand overnight.

2 Pour rind mixture into a colander set in a sink; rinse under cold running water; drain well. Transfer rind to a 4-quart heavy kettle or pot. Add enough cold water to cover. Heat to boiling; reduce heat. Simmer, covered, for 20 to 25 minutes or until rind is tender; drain.

3 Meanwhile, in a 6- to 8-quart stainless-steel, enamel, or nonstick kettle combine sugar, vinegar, the 1½ cups water, stick cinnamon, and cloves. Heat to boiling; reduce heat. Boil gently, uncovered, for 10 minutes. Strain liquid; return liquid to kettle. Add watermelon rind. Return to boiling; reduce heat. Simmer for 25 to 30 minutes or until rind is translucent.

4 Pack rind and syrup into hot, sterilized half-pint canning jars, leaving a ½-inch headspace. Wipe jar rims; adjust lids. Process filled jars in a boiling-water canner for 10 minutes (start timing when water returns to boil). Remove jars from canner; cool on wire racks.

PER ¼-CUP SERVING: 117 cal., 0 g total fat, 0 mg chol., 1,288 mg sodium, 27 g carbo., 0 g fiber, 0 g pro.

Hot and sweet peppers are combined in this delectably spicy condiment. Serve it alongside grilled steaks or chicken, on a burger, or tossed into potato and other salads.

HOT PICKLED SWEET PEPPERS

PREP: 1 HOUR **BAKE:** 20 MINUTES **PROCESS:** 15 MINUTES
OVEN: 450F° **MAKES:** 6 PINTS OR 12 HALF-PINTS (EIGHTY-FOUR 1/8-CUP SERVINGS)

4 1/2	pounds green, red, yellow, and/or orange sweet peppers
1 1/2	pounds hot chile peppers, such as Anaheim, jalapeño, yellow banana, or Hungarian*
6 1/2	cups white or cider vinegar
1 1/3	cups water
2/3	cup sugar
4	teaspoons pickling salt
3	cloves garlic, peeled

❶ Preheat oven to 450°F. Cut sweet peppers into quarters, removing stems, seeds, and membranes. Line an extra-large baking sheet with foil. Place sweet pepper quarters, cut sides down, on prepared baking sheet. Bake for 20 minutes or until skins are bubbly and dark. Place peppers in a clean brown paper bag; seal bag. Let stand for 10 minutes or until cool enough to handle. Using a paring knife, gently peel off skins; set sweet peppers aside.

❷ Remove stems and seeds from hot chile peppers. Slice into rings.

❸ In a large stainless-steel, enamel, or nonstick saucepan combine vinegar, water, sugar, pickling salt, and garlic. Heat to boiling; reduce heat. Simmer, uncovered, for 10 minutes. Remove garlic cloves.

❹ Pack sweet and hot peppers into hot, sterilized pint or half-pint canning jars, leaving a ½-inch headspace. Pour hot liquid over the peppers, leaving a ½-inch headspace. Wipe jar rims; adjust lids. Process filled jars in a boiling-water canner for 15 minutes (start timing when water returns to boil). Remove jars from canner; cool on wire racks.

*NOTE: Because chile peppers, such as jalapeños, contain oils that can burn skin and eyes, avoid direct contact with them as much as possible. Wear plastic or rubber gloves while preparing them. If your bare hands should touch a chile pepper, wash them well with soap and water.

PER 1/8-CUP SERVING: 28 cal., 0 g total fat, 0 mg chol., 180 mg sodium, 9 g carbo., 1 g fiber, 1 g pro.

Famously sweet Walla Walla onions are ideal for these crunchy rings, but other sweet onions, such as Vidalia, Maui, and Sweet Spanish, will give you equally delicious results.

WALLA WALLA PICKLED ONIONS

PREP: 2 ¼ HOURS **COOK:** 10 MINUTES **PROCESS:** 10 MINUTES **MAKES:** 7 PINTS (42 SERVINGS)

5 ½   **pounds sweet onions, such as Walla Walla**

4   **medium green or red sweet peppers**

4 ½   **cups cider vinegar**

⅔   **cup honey**

1   **teaspoon mustard seeds**

1   **teaspoon whole allspice**

½   **teaspoon anise seeds**

7   **bay leaves**

❶ Peel and slice enough onions ¼ inch thick to equal 22 cups when separated into rings. Remove seeds from peppers and slice into rings (you should have 6 cups loosely packed).

❷ In an 8- to 10-quart Dutch oven combine vinegar, honey, mustard seeds, allspice, and anise seeds; bring to boiling. Boil, uncovered, for 3 minutes. Add onion rings; cook and stir gently for 8 minutes or just until onions begin to turn limp.

❸ Remove from heat; stir in pepper rings. Add a bay leaf to each hot sterilized pint jar. Remove onions and peppers from Dutch oven with tongs and pack into hot, sterilized pint canning jars; ladle in vinegar mixture, leaving a ½-inch headspace. Wipe jar rims; adjust lids.

❹ Process in a boiling-water canner 10 minutes (start timing when water returns to boil). Remove jars from canner; cool on wire racks.

PER ¼-CUP SERVING: 37 cal., 0 g total fat, 0 mg chol., 2 mg sodium, 10 g carbo., 1 g fiber, 1 g pro.

This mustard-spiked mix of garden vegetables is believed to have been introduced to America by Chinese railroad workers. It adds a spark of flavor and crunch to almost any meal.

CHOW CHOW

PREP: 75 MINUTES **STAND:** OVERNIGHT **PROCESS:** 10 MINUTES **MAKES:** 6 PINTS (84 SERVINGS)

3   large onions, cut up

4   medium green tomatoes, cored and cut up

4   medium green sweet peppers, cut up

2   medium red sweet peppers, cut up

2   medium carrots, peeled and cut up

12   ounces green beans, cut into ½-inch pieces (2 cups)

2   cups small cauliflower florets

1½   cups fresh corn kernels (about 3 ears)

¼   cup pickling salt

3   cups sugar

2   cups vinegar

1   cup water

1   tablespoon mustard seeds

2   teaspoons grated fresh ginger (optional)

1½   teaspoons celery seeds

¾   teaspoon turmeric

1 Using a coarse blade of a food grinder, grind onions, tomatoes, green peppers, red peppers, and carrots. (Or use a food processor to process onions, tomatoes, green peppers, red peppers, and carrots in batches until finely chopped.) Transfer ground or chopped vegetables to an extra-large nonmetal bowl. Add green beans, cauliflower, and corn. Sprinkle with pickling salt; cover and let stand overnight.

2 Rinse and drain vegetable mixture. Transfer to an 8- to 10-quart heavy kettle or pot. Combine sugar, vinegar, water, mustard seeds, ginger (if desired), celery seeds, and turmeric; pour over vegetables. Bring mixture to boiling; boil gently for 5 minutes.

3 Ladle hot mixture into clean, hot, sterilized pint canning jars, leaving a ½-inch headspace. Wipe jar rims; adjust lids. Process filled jars in a boiling-water canner for 10 minutes (start timing when water returns to boil). Remove the jars from the canner; cool on wire racks.

PER 2-TABLESPOON SERVING : 40 cal., 0 g total fat, 0 mg chol., 156 mg sodium, 10 g carbo., 0 g pro.

These tasty tidbits are where the heat meets the sweet, making for a pickle that's downright addictive. Use them on sandwiches or on quesadillas, as toppers for grilled meats, or simply pop them into your mouth solo for a hit of fiery flavor.

SWEET JALAPEÑO SLICES

PREP: 25 MINUTES **CHILL:** 2 HOURS **PROCESS:** 15 MINUTES **MAKES:** 3 TO 4 HALF-PINTS (56 SERVINGS)

1 pound fresh jalapeño peppers, stemmed, halved, seeded, and cut into ½-inch slices*

1 large red sweet pepper, cut into ¼-inch strips

½ cup chopped onion (1 medium)

1 tablespoon pickling salt

Cracked ice

1¼ cups sugar

½ cup cider vinegar

1 teaspoon mustard seeds

½ teaspoon celery seeds

½ teaspoon ground turmeric

❶ In a large bowl combine jalapeño peppers, sweet pepper, onion, and pickling salt. Add 2 inches of cracked ice. Cover and chill for 2 hours.

❷ Remove any remaining ice. Drain mixture in a large colander.

❸ In a large stainless-steel, enamel, or nonstick saucepan combine sugar, vinegar, mustard seeds, celery seeds, and turmeric. Heat mixture to boiling. Stir in drained pepper mixture. Return to boiling. Ladle pepper mixture into hot, sterilized half-pint canning jars, leaving a ½-inch headspace. Wipe jar rims; adjust lids. Process in a boiling-water canner for 15 minutes (start timing when water returns to boil). Remove jars from canner; cool on wire racks.

*NOTE: Because chile peppers, such as jalapeños, contain oils that can burn skin and eyes, avoid direct contact with them as much as possible. Wear plastic or rubber gloves while preparing them. If bare hands should touch a chile pepper, wash them well with soap and water.

PER 1-TABLESPOON SERVING: 15 cal., 0 g total fat, 0 mg chol., 42 mg sodium, 3 g carbo., 0 g fiber, 0 g pro.

Chapter Four

RELISHES, SALSAS, SAUCES & CHUTNEYS

Make even simple meals special with homemade condiments. Pull out a jar of zesty relish, fiery salsa, piquant chutney, or flavor-infused sauce to make everyday sandwiches and grilled meats and fish something spectacular.

MAKING RELISHES, SALSAS, CHUTNEYS, AND SAUCES

Add layers of flavor with piquant and spicy condiments, made special with your own produce and by your own hands. Home-preserved condiments kick it up a notch at an everyday meal or impress special-occasion dinner guests with a thoughtful touch.

Whether you crave sweet, sour, tangy, spicy, or piquant—or maybe all of those things—home-canned condiments deliver. Merely opening a jar infuses foods with a burst of flavor. Make at-home gourmet condiments, such as Gingered Cranberry-Pear Chutney or Tomato-Basil Jam, which would be difficult to find or expensive in stores. Or add down-home flair to basic meals with Corn Relish, Zucchini Relish, or Rhubarb Sauce.

CONDIMENTS AND HOW TO USE THEM

RELISHES Usually pickled, relishes are most often made with pickles, onions, and other vegetables but sometimes include fruits. They range from smooth to chunky, sweet to savory, and spicy to mild.

Serving ideas: Relishes are excellent with any grilled meat, including hot dogs, sausages, chicken, fish, chops, and burgers. Try them spread on cold-cut sandwiches or stir them into potato, egg, or tuna salad.

SALSAS The Spanish word for sauce, salsa is usually spicy with onions, garlic, and Mexican-inspired flavors, such as lime and cilantro. It is most often tomato-based. However, there are many variations, such as cucumber salsas and fruit-based salsas of pineapple and mango.

Serving ideas: Pair with tortilla chips and a flavorful topper for nearly any Mexican dish. Also spoon salsa on sandwiches or baked

potatoes. Stir into or drizzle on top of dips. Stir in a spoonful or two to enliven a soup, casserole, or pot of rice. Great on plain meats and with cheese. Fruit salsas are delicious with fish.

CHUTNEYS These sweet-sour condiments are inspired by the flavors of India and are usually a combination of vegetables and fruits, spices, and vinegar cooked for a long time to develop deep flavor.

Serving ideas: Add another layer of flavor to Indian and some Asian foods. Or put out a bowl with cheese and crackers for an interesting appetizer. Stir into or drizzle on top of dips. Excellent to perk up plain beef, pork, and chicken. Holiday versions are custom-made for turkey and ham.

SAUCES If it can be harvested from the garden, it likely has been turned into a sauce of some sort. Home-canned sauces include savory versions, such as ketchup, chili sauce, hot sauce, or barbeque sauce. Or they can be a combination of sweet and sour, such as cherry or plum sauce designed to serve with meats.

Sauces can also be sweet and basic, such as rhubarb sauce, or delicious syrups made from berries.

Serving ideas: Serve savory sauces with savory foods. Sweet sauces are great over pound or angel food cakes, plain cheesecakes, ice creams, and pancakes.

CONDIMENTS TROUBLESHOOTING

PROBLEM	CAUSE	SOLUTION
Foods become black, brown, or gray in the jar.	Natural substances in the foods may be reacting with metal kitchen tools or hard water.	Use soft water for canning foods. Use nonmetallic, nonreactive pans, bowls, and utensils. If there is any sign of spoilage or an odd or unpleasant odor, discard.
Jar seals properly after processing but comes unsealed during storage.	Food could be spoiling and gases expanding, or the lid wasn't put on properly, or too much air remained in the jar after processing. (Never use a jar that has come open, even if it looks and smells safe.)	Use a current, reliable recipe and process for the recommended period of time. Follow exactly the instructions on page 32 for putting on lids. Make sure you are precise in creating the headspace specified in the recipe. Always slide a nonmetallic thin spatula around the sides of the filled jar before putting on the lid to get out air bubbles.
Loss of liquid during processing.	Too much air was in the jar before processing or processing wasn't done correctly.	Add the correct amount of liquid, as directed, during raw-pack recipes and measure headspace carefully. Or use a hot-pack method recipe, which assures less air in the jar. Always slide a nonmetallic thin spatula around the sides of the filled jar before putting on the lid to get out air bubbles. Make sure boiling-water process jars are covered with 1 to 2 inches of water at all times during timing. Keep pressure consistent during pressure canning.

If you have too much of this tongue-tingling relish to fit in the jars, refrigerate the extra in a covered container and use it within 2 weeks.

SWEET PICKLE RELISH

PREP: 1 HOUR **STAND:** 2 HOURS **COOK:** 10 MINUTES **PROCESS:** 10 MINUTES
MAKES: 7 HALF-PINTS (98 SERVINGS)

6   medium unwaxed cucumbers

3   green and/or red sweet peppers

6   medium onions

¼   cup pickling salt

3   cups sugar

2   cups cider vinegar

2½ teaspoons celery seeds

2½ teaspoons mustard seeds

½   teaspoon turmeric

1 Wash cucumbers and peppers. Chop; discard pepper stems, membranes, and seeds. If desired, seed cucumbers. Measure 6 cups cucumber and 3 cups sweet peppers. Peel and chop onions; measure 3 cups chopped onions. Combine vegetables in a large bowl. Sprinkle with pickling salt; add cold water to cover. Let stand, covered, at room temperature for 2 hours.

2 Pour vegetable mixture into colander set in sink. Rinse with fresh water and drain well.

3 In a 4-quart kettle or pot combine sugar, vinegar, celery seeds, mustard seeds, and turmeric. Heat to boiling. Add drained vegetable mixture; return to boiling. Cook, uncovered, over medium-high heat about 10 minutes or until most of the excess liquid has evaporated, stirring occasionally.

4 Ladle relish into hot, sterilized half-pint canning jars, leaving a ½-inch headspace. Wipe the jar rims; adjust lids. Process filled jars in a boiling-water canner for 10 minutes (start timing when water returns to boil). Remove the jars from the canner; cool on wire racks.

PER 1-TABLESPOON SERVING: 29 cal., 0 g total fat, 0 mg chol, 131 mg sodium, 7 g carbo., 0 g fiber, 0 g pro.

If you're lucky enough to have fresh corn for this classic relish, by all means use it. But if fresh isn't readily available, substitute frozen whole kernel corn.

CORN RELISH

PREP: 1½ HOURS **COOK:** 12 MINUTES **PROCESS:** 15 MINUTES **MAKES:** ABOUT 5 PINTS (70 SERVINGS)

12	to 16 fresh ears of corn
2	cups water
3	cups chopped celery (6 stalks)
1½	cups chopped red sweet peppers (2)
1½	cups chopped green sweet peppers (2)
1	cup chopped onions (2 medium)
2½	cups vinegar
1¾	cups sugar
4	teaspoons dry mustard
2	teaspoons pickling salt
2	teaspoons celery seeds
1	teaspoon ground turmeric
3	tablespoons cornstarch
2	tablespoons water

❶ Remove husks and silks from corn; cut corn from cobs (do not scrape cobs). Measure 8 cups of corn. In an 8- to 10-quart stainless-steel, enamel, or nonstick heavy kettle or pot combine corn and the 2 cups water. Bring to boiling; reduce heat. Simmer, covered, for 4 to 5 minutes or until corn is nearly tender; drain.

❷ In the same kettle, combine cooked corn, celery, red and green sweet peppers, and onions. Stir in vinegar, sugar, mustard, pickling salt, celery seeds, and turmeric. Bring to boiling. Boil gently, uncovered, for 5 minutes, stirring occasionally. Stir together cornstarch and the 2 tablespoons water; add to corn mixture. Cook and stir until slightly thickened and bubbly; cook and stir for 2 minutes more.

❸ Ladle hot relish into hot, sterilized pint canning jars, leaving a ½-inch headspace. Wipe jar rims; adjust lids. Process filled jars in a boiling-water canner for 15 minutes (start timing when water returns to boil). Remove the jars from canner; cool on wire racks.

PER 2-TABLESPOON SERVING: 40 cal., 0 g total fat, 0 mg chol., 73 mg sodium, 9 g carbo., 1 g fiber, 1 g pro.

RELISHES, SALSAS, SAUCES & CHUTNEYS

Do more with all that zucchini besides give it to the neighbors. Make this delectable, tangy relish and you'll want to keep it all to yourself!

ZUCCHINI RELISH

PREP: 1 HOUR **STAND:** 3 HOURS **COOK:** 15 MINUTES **PROCESS:** 10 MINUTES
MAKES: 5 HALF-PINTS (80 SERVINGS)

5	cups finely chopped zucchini
1 1/2	cups finely chopped onions (3 medium)
3/4	cup finely chopped green sweet pepper (1 medium)
3/4	cup finely chopped red sweet pepper (1 medium)
1/4	cup pickling salt
1 3/4	cups sugar
1 1/2	cups white vinegar
1/4	cup water
1	teaspoon celery seeds
1	teaspoon ground turmeric
1/2	teaspoon mustard seeds
1	or 2 drops green food coloring (optional)

❶ In a large nonmetal bowl combine zucchini, onions, and green and red sweet peppers. Sprinkle the pickling salt over vegetables. Add enough water (about 4 cups) to cover vegetables. Cover; let stand for 3 hours.

❷ Drain zucchini mixture in a large colander set in sink. Rinse under running water; drain well.

❸ In an 8- or 10-quart stainless-steel, enamel, or nonstick kettle or pot combine sugar, vinegar, the 1/4 cup water, the celery seeds, turmeric, and mustard seeds. Heat to boiling; reduce heat. Simmer, uncovered, for 3 minutes. Stir in drained zucchini mixture and, if desired, green food coloring. Return to boiling; reduce heat. Simmer, uncovered, for 10 minutes.

❹ Ladle relish into hot, sterilized half-pint canning jars, leaving a 1/2-inch headspace. Wipe jar rims; adjust lids. Process filled jars in a boiling water canner for 10 minutes (start timing when water returns to boil.) Remove jars from canner; cool on wire racks.

PER 1-TABLESPOON SERVING: 48 cal., 0 g total fat, 0 mg chol., 134 mg sodium, 11 g carbo., 0 g fiber, 0 g pro.

You need only the peeled rind of the watermelon for this Louisiana favorite. It's a natural with grilled hot dogs and spicy sausages, but also try it with grilled shrimp or other fish for a treat straight from the bayou.

CAJUN WATERMELON RELISH

PREP: 30 MINUTES **CHILL:** 8 HOURS **COOK:** 25 MINUTES **MAKES:** 3 HALF-PINTS

½ of a 12- to 14-pound watermelon

1 cup water

1 tablespoon pickling salt

½ teaspoon pickling spice

1 cup vinegar

½ cup sugar

1 teaspoon crushed red pepper

1½ cups chopped assorted red, yellow, and/or green sweet peppers (2 medium)

1 cup chopped onion (1 large)

1 small jalapeño pepper, seeded, if desired, and thinly sliced*

❶ Cut pink flesh from watermelon. Refrigerate and save for another use. Using a vegetable peeler, remove green peel from rind; discard peel. Dice rind. Measure 2 cups rind; place in a large bowl.

❷ Combine the 1 cup water and pickling salt; pour over rind. Cover bowl and refrigerate at least 8 hours.

❸ Pour the rind into a colander set in a sink. Rinse under cold running water; drain well.

❹ Make a spice bag by placing pickling spice on a double thickness of 6-inch squares of cotton cheesecloth. Tie corners together with kitchen string.

❺ In a 4-quart stainless-steel, enamel, or nonstick heavy kettle or pot combine pickling spice bag, vinegar, sugar, and crushed red pepper. Heat to boiling, stirring to dissolve sugar. Stir in diced watermelon rind, sweet peppers, onion, and jalapeño pepper. Return to boiling; reduce heat. Simmer, covered, over medium-low heat about 25 minutes or until rind is transparent. Discard spice bag.

❻ Pack hot relish into hot, sterilized half-pint canning jars, leaving a ½-inch headspace. Wipe jar rims; adjust lids. Process filled jars in a boiling-water canner for 10 minutes (start timing when water returns to boil). Remove jars from canner; cool on wire racks.

*NOTE: Because chile peppers, contain oils that can burn skin and eyes, avoid direct contact with them as much as possible. Wear plastic or rubber gloves while preparing them. If your bare hands should touch a chile pepper, wash well with soap and water.

PER 2-TABLESPOON SERVING: 26 cal., 0 g total fat, 0 mg chol., 25 mg sodium, 7 g carbo., 0 g fiber, 0 g pro.

Serve this with grilled hot dogs or sausages at your next summer barbecue or shelve it to give as holiday gifts.

GREEN TOMATO RELISH

PREP: 1 HOUR **CHILL:** 8HOURS **PROCESS:** 10 MINUTES
MAKES: 6 TO 7 HALF-PINTS OR 3 TO 4 PINTS (84 SERVINGS)

2	pounds green tomatoes, cored (6 medium)
8	ounces cabbage, cored
3	medium green sweet peppers, quartered and seeded
2	medium red sweet peppers, quartered and seeded
1	large onion
2	tablespoons pickling salt
1¼	cups sugar
1¼	cups cider vinegar
½	cup water
2	teaspoons mustard seeds
1	teaspoon celery seeds
½	teaspoon ground turmeric

❶ Use a food processor to finely chop green tomatoes, cabbage, green and red sweet peppers, and onion, processing a portion at a time, using several on/off turns of the processor. (Or finely chop by hand.) You need 4 cups chopped tomatoes, 3 cups chopped cabbage, 2¼ cups chopped green peppers, 1½ cups chopped red peppers, and 1 cup chopped onion. Place vegetables in a large bowl. Sprinkle with the 2 tablespoons pickling salt; stir well. Cover and refrigerate at least 8 hours.

❷ Drain vegetable mixture in a large colander set in the sink. Rinse well under running water; drain well.

❸ In a 6- to 8-quart stainless-steel, enamel, or nonstick kettle or pot combine sugar, vinegar, water, mustard seeds, celery seeds, and turmeric. Heat to boiling, stirring to dissolve sugar. Add vegetable mixture. Return to boiling, stirring frequently. Remove from heat.

❹ Ladle hot relish into hot, sterilized half-pint or pint canning jars, leaving a ½-inch headspace. Wipe jar rims; adjust lids. Process filled jars in a boiling-water canner for 5 minutes for half-pints or 10 minutes for pints (start timing when water returns to boil). Remove jars from canner; cool on wire racks.

PER 1-TABLESPOON SERVING: 15 cal., 0 g total fat, 0 mg chol., 68 mg sodium, 4 g carbo., 0 g fiber, 0 g pro.

RELISHES, SALSAS, SAUCES & CHUTNEYS

Anaheim and poblano chiles are mild peppers that add flavor and texture to this salsa. The jalapeños or serranos provide the heat. Use more serranos and fewer jalapeños for the maximum amount of fire.

CHUNKY HOMEMADE SALSA

PREP: 1 HOUR **STAND:** 30 MINUTES **COOK:** 70 MINUTES **PROCESS:** 15 MINUTES
MAKES: 5 PINTS (140 SERVINGS)

7 pounds tomatoes (about 20)

10 Anaheim or poblano chile peppers*

3 jalapeño or serrano chile peppers*

2 cups chopped onions (2 large)

1 cup vinegar

½ cup snipped fresh cilantro or parsley

½ of a 6-ounce can tomato paste (⅓ cup)

1 tablespoon sugar

1 teaspoon salt

1 teaspoon black pepper

5 cloves garlic, minced

❶ Wash tomatoes. Remove peels, stem ends, cores, and seeds. Coarsely chop tomatoes. Measure 14 cups. Place in a large colander. Let drain for 30 minutes. Place drained tomatoes in an 8-quart stainless-steel, enamel, or nonstick kettle or pot. Heat to boiling; reduce heat. Simmer, uncovered, for 1 to 1¼ hours or until thickened, stirring frequently.

❷ Meanwhile, seed and chop Anaheim or poblano chile peppers; measure 3 cups. Seed and chop jalapeño or serrano chile peppers; measure ⅓ cup. Add chile peppers, onions, vinegar, cilantro, tomato paste, sugar, salt, black pepper, and garlic to tomatoes. Return mixture to boiling; reduce heat. Simmer, uncovered, for 10 minutes. Remove from heat.

❸ Ladle hot salsa into hot, sterilized pint canning jars, leaving a ½-inch headspace. Wipe jar rims; adjust lids. Process filled jars in a boiling-water canner for 15 minutes (start timing when water returns to boil). Remove jars from canner; cool on wire racks.

*NOTE: Because chile peppers contain oils that can burn skin and eyes, avoid direct contact with them as much as possible. Wear plastic or rubber gloves while preparing them. If your bare hands should touch a chile pepper, wash them well with soap and water.

PER 1-TABLESPOON SERVING: 10 cal., 0 g total fat, 0 mg chol., 25 mg sodium, 2 g carbo., 1 g fiber, 1 g pro.

This summer-in-a-jar salsa is a tasty dip to serve with tortilla chips. Try it as a topper on simple grilled pork, beef, chicken, and fish as well.

FARMER'S MARKET CORN SALSA

PREP: 35 MINUTES **COOK:** 10 MINUTES **PROCESS:** 15 MINUTES
MAKES: ABOUT 4 HALF-PINTS (16 SERVINGS)

4	large ears fresh corn
1	cup coarsely chopped onion (1 large)
1	cup coarsely chopped green or red sweet pepper (1 large)
1	large tomato, peeled and chopped (1 cup)
1	fresh jalapeño chile pepper, seeded and finely chopped*
½	cup fresh lime juice
½	teaspoon salt
½	teaspoon ground cumin
½	teaspoon freshly ground black pepper

❶ Remove husks from the ears of corn. Scrub with a stiff brush to remove silks; rinse. Cut corn from cobs.

❷ In a large saucepan combine corn, onion, sweet pepper, tomato, jalapeño, lime juice, salt, cumin, and black pepper. Bring to boiling over medium-high heat. Reduce heat and simmer, covered, for 10 minutes. Transfer to hot, sterilized half-pint jars, leaving a ½-inch headspace. Wipe jar rims; adjust lids.

❸ Process in a boiling-water canner for 15 minutes (start timing when water returns to boil). Remove jars from canner; cool on wire racks.

*NOTE: Because chile peppers, such as jalapeños, contain oils that can burn your skin and eyes, avoid direct contact with them as much as possible. Wear plastic or rubber gloves while preparing them. If your bare hands should touch a chile pepper, wash them well with soap and water.

PER ¼-CUP SERVING: 48 cal., 1 g total fat (0 g sat. fat), 0 mg chol., 0 mg sodium, 11 g carbo., 2 g fiber, 2 g pro.

Tomatillos have a lemony flavor and crisp texture. Tart Granny Smith apples are an ideal choice to round out the flavor of this fruity salsa.

TOMATILLO-APPLE SALSA

PREP: 45 MINUTES **COOK:** 15 MINUTES **PROCESS:** 10 MINUTES
MAKES: 4 TO 5 HALF-PINTS (56 SERVINGS)

24	fresh tomatillos (about 2 pounds)
2	cups finely chopped, peeled tart apples (3 medium)
½	cup chopped red sweet pepper
½	cup cider vinegar
4	to 6 fresh jalapeño chile peppers, seeded and finely chopped (¼ to ⅓ cup)*
¼	cup snipped fresh cilantro
¼	cup sugar
1	teaspoon salt

1 Remove the husks from the tomatillos. Wash the fruit well in cold water. Cut the tomatillos in half and remove the cores. Chop the tomatillos. Measure 4 cups chopped tomatillos.

2 In a 4- to 6-quart stainless-steel, enamel, or nonstick kettle or pot combine tomatillos, apples, sweet peppers, jalapeño peppers, cilantro, sugar, and salt. Heat to boiling; reduce heat. Simmer, uncovered, for 15 minutes.

3 Ladle hot salsa into hot, sterilized half-pint canning jars, leaving a ½-inch headspace. Wipe jar rims; adjust lids. Process filled jars in a boiling-water canner for 10 minutes (start timing when water returns to boil). Remove jars from canner; cool on wire racks.

*NOTE: Because chile peppers, such as jalapeños, contain oils that can burn skin and eyes, avoid direct contact with them as much as possible. Wear plastic or rubber gloves while preparing them. If your bare hands should touch a chile pepper, wash well with soap and water.

PER 1-TABLESPOON SERVING: 12 cal., 0 g total fat, 0 mg chol., 42 mg sodium, 3 g carbo., 0 g fiber, 0 g pro.

There are more things to do with blueberries than put them in muffins or make them into jam. This unusual chutney dresses up plain ham, roasted chicken, turkey, and beef.

BLUEBERRY CHUTNEY

PREP: 10 MINUTES **COOK:** 55 MINUTES **PROCESS:** 10 MINUTES
MAKES: 3 HALF-PINTS (24 SERVINGS)

1	cup sugar
1	cup raspberry-flavored vinegar
1	cup finely chopped onion (1 large)
2	teaspoons finely shredded lemon peel
1/2	teaspoon grated fresh ginger
1/4	teaspoon ground cinnamon
1/8	teaspoon salt
1/8	teaspoon cayenne pepper
6	cups fresh or frozen blueberries
1	cup fresh or frozen cranberries

❶ In a medium saucepan stir together sugar, vinegar, onion, lemon peel, ginger, cinnamon, salt, and cayenne pepper. Heat to boiling, stirring to dissolve sugar; reduce heat. Simmer, uncovered, for 15 minutes, stirring occasionally.

❷ Stir in 2 cups of the blueberries and the cranberries. Return to boiling; reduce heat. Simmer, uncovered, for 20 minutes, stirring occasionally.

❸ Add remaining 4 cups blueberries. Return to boiling; reduce heat. Simmer, uncovered, for 20 minutes more or until thickened and of desired consistency, stirring occasionally.

❹ Ladle hot chutney into hot, sterilized half-pint canning jars, leaving a ½-inch headspace. Wipe jar rims; adjust lids. Process filled jars in a boiling-water canner for 10 minutes (start timing when water returns to boil). Remove jars from canner; cool on wire racks. (Or ladle mixture into half-pint freezer containers; seal and label. Store up to 2 weeks in the refrigerator or up to 3 months in the freezer.)

PER 2-TABLESPOON SERVING: 58 cal., 0 g total fat, 0 mg chol., 13 mg sodium, 15 g carbo., 1 g fiber, 0 g pro.

Fruits and aromatic spices team up for a chutney that's delicious as a side to cheese and crackers, with chicken, or alongside ham.

PEAR-CHERRY CHUTNEY

PREP: 30 MINUTES **COOK:** 20 MINUTES **PROCESS:** 10 MINUTES **MAKES:** 4 HALF-PINTS (32 SERVINGS)

1 cup dried tart red cherries, snipped

½ cup sugar

2 teaspoons finely shredded lemon peel

⅓ cup lemon juice

½ teaspoon ground cinnamon

½ teaspoon ground allspice

5 cups coarsely chopped, peeled ripe pears*

1 In a heavy kettle or pot combine dried cherries, sugar, lemon peel, lemon juice, cinnamon, and allspice. Heat to boiling over high heat; reduce heat to medium. Simmer, uncovered, for 5 minutes, stirring occasionally. Stir in pears; return to boiling. Simmer, covered, for 10 minutes. Simmer, uncovered, about 5 minutes more or until cooking liquid barely covers fruit.

2 Ladle hot chutney into hot, sterilized half-pint canning jars, leaving a ½-inch headspace. Wipe jar rims; adjust lids. Process filled jars in a boiling-water canner for 10 minutes (start timing when water returns to boil). Remove jars from canner; cool in wire racks. (Or ladle into half-pint freezer containers, leaving a ½-inch headspace. Seal and label. Store up to 2 weeks in the refrigerator or up to 6 months in the freezer.)

*NOTE: Place peeled, cored, and cut-up pears in a food processor one-third at a time. Pulse to coarsely chop.

PER 2-TABLESPOON SERVING: 41 cal., 0 g total fat, 0 mg chol., 0 mg sodium, 11 g carbo., 1 g fiber, 0 g pro.

Top a wheel of Brie cheese—warmed in the oven or served at room temperature—with this jewel-tone chutney. It makes a lovely appetizer for a holiday party. In the jar it makes a colorful and welcome gift.

GINGERED CRANBERRY-PEAR CHUTNEY

PREP: 30 MINUTES **COOK:** 35 MINUTES **PROCESS:** 10 MINUTES **MAKES:** 5 HALF-PINTS (40 SERVINGS)

1	12-ounce package fresh cranberries (3 cups)
1²/₃	cups packed brown sugar
½	cup chopped onion (1 medium)
1⅓	cups water
½	cup cider vinegar
1	tablespoon lemon juice
3	inches stick cinnamon
1	tablespoon grated fresh ginger
3	cups coarsely chopped, peeled pears (3 medium)

❶ In a 4-quart kettle or pot combine cranberries, brown sugar, and onion. Stir in water, vinegar, lemon juice, stick cinnamon, and ginger. Heat to boiling; reduce heat to low. Simmer, uncovered, for 20 minutes. Add pears. Simmer, uncovered, about 15 minutes more or until thick. Discard stick cinnamon.

❷ Ladle hot chutney into hot, sterilized half-pint canning jars, leaving a ½-inch headspace. Wipe jar rims; adjust lids. Process filled jars in a boiling-water canner for 10 minutes (start timing when water returns to boil). Remove jars from canner; cool on wire racks. (Or ladle chutney into half-pint freezer containers, leaving a ½-inch headspace. Seal and label. Store up to 2 weeks in the refrigerator or up to 6 months in the freezer.)

PER 2-TABLESPOON SERVING: 48 cal., 0 g total fat, 0 mg chol., 3 mg sodium, 12 g carbo., 1 g fiber, 0 g pro.

Serve this sweet and savory condiment with grilled beef or chicken, spread it on a cold pork sandwich, or pair it with a sharp aged cheddar or Gouda and crackers for a party snack.

TOMATO-RHUBARB CHUTNEY

PREP: 20 MINUTES **COOK:** 40 MINUTES **PROCESS:** 10 MINUTES **MAKES:** 3 HALF-PINTS (24 SERVINGS)

1½ **cups chopped, seeded tomatoes (3 medium)**

⅓ **cup chopped onion (1 small)**

⅓ **cup coarsely chopped red sweet pepper**

⅓ **cup dried cherries, dried cranberries, or raisins**

⅓ **cup white vinegar**

¼ **cup granulated sugar**

¼ **cup packed brown sugar**

¼ **cup water**

1 **tablespoon lime or lemon juice**

1 **teaspoon grated fresh ginger or ¼ teaspoon ground ginger**

¼ **teaspoon salt**

2 **cloves garlic, minced**

1 **cup fresh ½-inch pieces rhubarb or 1 cup frozen cut rhubarb, thawed and drained**

1 In a large saucepan combine tomatoes, onion, sweet pepper, dried fruit, vinegar, granulated sugar, brown sugar, water, lime juice, ginger, salt, and garlic. Heat to boiling; reduce heat. Simmer, covered, for 25 minutes, stirring occasionally.

2 Stir rhubarb into tomato mixture. Simmer, covered, for 10 minutes. Uncover; simmer about 5 minutes more (15 minutes more, if using frozen rhubarb) or until thickened.

3 Ladle hot chutney into hot, sterilized half-pint canning jars, leaving a ½-inch headspace. Wipe jar rims; adjust lids. Process filled jars in a boiling-water canner for 10 minutes (start timing when water returns to boil). Remove jars from canner; cool on wire racks. (Or ladle chutney into half-pint freezer containers, leaving a ½-inch headspace. Seal and label. Store up to 1 week in the refrigerator or up to 3 months in the freezer.)

PER 2 -TABLESPOON SERVING: 30 cal., 0 g total fat, 0 mg chol., 29 mg sodium, 8 g carbo., 0 g fiber, 0 g pro.

Southern cooks have the right idea: They complement simple easy-to-roast meats, such as ham, with make-ahead or quick-to-fix relishes, pickles, and condiments, such as this peachy chutney. This strategy lightens prep work—and serves up a special touch with a home-canned treat.

PEACH CHUTNEY

PREP: 30 MINUTES **COOK:** 15 MINUTES **PROCESS:** 10 MINUTES **MAKES:** 4 HALF-PINTS (32 SERVINGS)

1 tablespoon vegetable oil

1 cup chopped onions (2 medium)

2 teaspoons grated fresh ginger

4 cloves garlic, minced

2/3 cup sugar

1/2 cup red wine vinegar

1/4 cup lemon juice

1/2 teaspoon dry mustard

1/2 teaspoon ground allspice

Dash ground cloves

3 cups chopped, peeled peaches (4 medium)

3/4 cup dried tart red cherries or raisins

❶ In a medium saucepan heat oil over medium heat. Add onions, ginger, and garlic; cook until onions are tender but not browned.

❷ Stir sugar, vinegar, lemon juice, mustard, allspice, and cloves into onion mixture. Bring to boiling, stirring to dissolve sugar. Reduce heat. Simmer, uncovered, for 5 minutes. Stir in peaches and cherries. Return to boiling; reduce heat. Simmer, uncovered, about 10 minutes or until thickened, stirring occasionally.

❸ Ladle hot chutney into hot, sterilized half-pint canning jars, leaving a ½-inch headspace. Wipe jar rims; adjust lids. Process filled jars in a boiling-water canner for 10 minutes (start timing when water returns to boil). Remove jars from canner; cool on wire racks. (Or ladle cooled chutney into half-pint freezer containers, leaving a ½-inch headspace. Seal and label. Store up to 2 weeks in the refrigerator or up to 6 months in the freezer.)

PER 2-TABLESPOON SERVING: 39 cal., 0 g total fat, 0 mg chol., 1 mg sodium, 9 g carbo., 1 g fiber, 0 g pro.

Here's a neat trick: Determine that the tomato-sugar mixture is reduced by half by measuring its depth with a clean ruler at the beginning and near the end of simmering.

KETCHUP

PREP: 3 HOURS **COOK:** 2½ HOURS **PROCESS:** 15 MINUTES **MAKES:** 4 HALF-PINTS

8 **pounds tomatoes (24 medium)**

½ **cup chopped onion (1 medium)**

¼ **teaspoon cayenne pepper**

¾ **cup sugar**

1 **cup white vinegar**

1½ **inches stick cinnamon, broken**

1½ **teaspoons whole cloves**

1 **teaspoon celery seeds**

1 **tablespoon salt**

1 Core and quarter tomatoes; drain. In an 8- to 10-quart stainless-steel, enamel, or nonstick heavy kettle or pot combine tomatoes, onion, and cayenne pepper. Heat to boiling. Cook, covered, for 15 minutes, stirring often.

2 Press tomato mixture through a food mill or sieve. Discard seeds and skins. Return tomato mixture to kettle; stir in sugar. Heat to boiling; reduce heat. Simmer, uncovered, for 1½ to 2 hours or until reduced by half, stirring occasionally.

3 In a small stainless steel, enamel, or nonstick saucepan combine vinegar, cinnamon, cloves, and celery seeds. Heat to boiling. Remove from heat. Strain vinegar mixture into tomato mixture; discard spices. Add salt. Simmer, uncovered, about 30 minutes or to desired consistency, stirring often. Can or freeze ketchup as directed below.

TO CAN: Ladle hot ketchup into hot, sterilized half-pint canning jars, leaving a ½-inch headspace. Wipe jar rims; adjust lids. Process in a boiling-water canner for 15 minutes (start timing when water returns to boil). Remove jars from canner; cool on wire racks.

TO FREEZE: Place kettle in a sink filled with ice water; stir mixture to cool. Ladle ketchup into half-pint freezer containers, leaving a ½-inch headspace. Seal and label. Store in the freezer for up to 10 months.

PER 1-TABLESPOON SERVING: 21 cal., 0 g total fat (0 g sat. fat), 0 mg chol., 114 mg sodium, 5 g carbo., 1 g fiber, 0 g pro.

Slather this tasty spread on warm focaccia or savory scones for an easy appetizer or use it to pump up the flavor of a salami or grilled cheese sandwich.

TOMATO-BASIL JAM

PREP: 30 MINUTES **COOK:** 12 MINUTES **PROCESS:** 5 MINUTES
MAKES: 5 HALF-PINTS (70 SERVINGS)

2 ½	**pounds fully ripe tomatoes (5 large red, yellow, or a mix)**
¼	**cup bottled lemon juice**
3	**tablespoons snipped fresh basil**
3	**cups sugar**
1	**1.75-ounce package powdered fruit pectin for lower-sugar recipes**

1 Wash tomatoes. Remove skins (see page 34), stem ends, cores, and seeds. Finely chop tomatoes. Measure 3½ cups. Place chopped tomatoes in a 6- or 8-quart kettle or pot. Heat to boiling; reduce heat. Simmer, covered, for 10 minutes. Measure 3⅓ cups; return to kettle.

2 Add lemon juice and basil. Combine ¼ cup of the sugar with the pectin; stir into tomato mixture. Heat to a full rolling boil, stirring constantly. Stir in the remaining 2¾ cups sugar. Return mixture to a full rolling boil. Boil hard for 1 minute, stirring constantly. Remove from heat. Quickly skim off foam with a metal spoon.

3 Immediately ladle hot jam into hot, sterilized half-pint canning jars, leaving a ¼-inch headspace. Wipe jar rims; adjust lids.

4 Process filled jars in a boiling-water canner for 5 minutes (start timing when water returns to boil). Remove jars from canner; cool on wire racks.

PER 1-TABLESPOON SERVING: 39 cal., 0 g total fat, 0 mg chol., 4 mg sodium, 10 g carbo., 0 g fiber, 0 g pro.

Looking for a new way to work cranberries into a holiday meal? Try this lime- and jalapeño-spiked cranberry sauce to liven up the traditional ham, lamb, turkey, or beef.

HOLIDAY CRANBERRY SAUCE

PREP: 40 MINUTES **COOK:** 45 MINUTES **PROCESS:** 5 MINUTES
MAKES: ABOUT 6 HALF-PINTS (40 SERVINGS)

4   cups fresh cranberries, coarsely chopped

2   cups sugar

1   teaspoon finely shredded orange peel

1¾   cups orange juice

½   cup chopped yellow sweet pepper

½   cup chopped red onion

½   cup honey

2   fresh jalapeño peppers, seeded and finely chopped*

1   teaspoon finely shredded lime peel

¼   cup lime juice

½   teaspoon salt

2   large oranges, peeled, sectioned, and cut up (about 1 cup)

① In a large heavy saucepan combine cranberries, sugar, orange peel, orange juice, sweet pepper, red onion, honey, jalapeños, lime peel, lime juice, and salt. Bring to boiling over medium-high heat, stirring to dissolve sugar. Mixture may foam when it boils, which will decrease as it cooks. Continue boiling at a moderate, steady rate for about 45 minutes or until mixture is thickened and reduced to about 4¼ cups, stirring frequently. Remove from heat and stir in oranges.

② Ladle at once into hot, sterilized half-pint canning jars, leaving a ¼-inch headspace. Wipe jar rims and adjust lids. Process in a boiling-water canner for 5 minutes (start timing when water returns to a boil). Remove jars and cool on racks until cool.

NOTE: Because hot chile peppers, such as jalapeños, contain volatile oils that can burn skin and eyes, avoid direct contact with chiles as much as possible. When working with chile peppers, wear plastic or rubber gloves. If your bare hands do touch the chile peppers, wash well with soap and water.

PER 2-TABLESPOON SERVING: 68 cal., 0 g total fat, 0 mg chol., 30 mg sodium, 17 g carbo., 1 g fiber, 0 g pro.

Brush this glossy sauce on ribs, chicken, or brisket for cooking on the grill outdoors or inside in the oven.

SPICY BARBECUE SAUCE

PREP: 1 HOUR **COOK:** 2 HOURS **PROCESS:** 20 MINUTES **MAKES:** 5 HALF-PINTS (70 SERVINGS)

12	pounds ripe firm tomatoes
3	cups chopped onions (3 large)
2 1/4	cups chopped celery (6 to 7 stalks)
2 1/4	cups chopped red or green sweet peppers (3 medium)
3	red hot chile peppers, cored and chopped*
3	cloves garlic, crushed
2	cups vinegar
1 1/2	cups packed brown sugar
3	tablespoons Worcestershire sauce
4	teaspoons paprika
4	teaspoons salt
4	teaspoons dry mustard
1/2	teaspoon black pepper

1 Wash tomatoes. Remove stem ends and cores. Cut tomatoes into quarters.

2 Place tomato quarters in a 10- to 12-quart kettle or pot. Cook, covered, over low to medium heat about 15 minutes or until tomatoes are soft. Add onions, celery, sweet peppers, chile peppers, and garlic. Heat to boiling; reduce heat. Simmer, uncovered, for 30 minutes.

3 Press tomato mixture through a food mill. Discard seeds and skins. Measure 19 cups. Return tomato mixture to kettle. Measure and note depth of mixture with a ruler. Heat to boiling; reduce heat. Simmer, uncovered, for 1 to 1¼ hours or until mixture is reduced by half, stirring occasionally. Depth of mixture should be half of the original measure.

4 Stir in vinegar, brown sugar, Worcestershire sauce, paprika, salt, mustard, and pepper. Simmer, uncovered, over low to medium heat about 1 hour or until desired thickness, stirring frequently.

5 Ladle hot sauce into hot, sterilized half-pint canning jars, leaving a ½-inch headspace. Wipe jar rims; adjust lids. Process filled jars in a boiling-water canner for 20 minutes (start timing when water returns to boil). Remove jars from canner; cool on wire racks.

*NOTE: Because chile peppers contain oils that can burn skin and eyes, avoid direct contact with them as much as possible. Wear plastic or rubber gloves while preparing them. If your bare hands should touch a chile pepper, wash well with soap and water.

PER 1-TABLESPOON SERVING: 38 cal., 0 g total fat, 0 mg chol., 142 mg sodium, 9 g carbo., 1 g fiber, 1 g pro.

When a recipe calls for chili sauce, stir in this home-canned version. Or serve it as a lively topping for meat loaf and other meats.

HOT-STYLE CHILI SAUCE

PREP: 45 MINUTES **COOK:** 2 HOURS **PROCESS:** 15 MINUTES **MAKES:** 7 HALF-PINTS (98 SERVINGS)

6	pounds tomatoes
1	cup finely chopped onion (1 large)
2	cups cider vinegar
1/2	cup sugar
1/3	cup chili powder
2	teaspoons salt
1	teaspoon dry mustard
1/4	to 1/2 teaspoon cayenne pepper

1 Wash tomatoes. Remove peels, stem ends, and cores. Chop tomatoes. In a 6- or 8-quart kettle or pot combine the chopped tomatoes, onion, vinegar, sugar, chili powder, salt, mustard, and cayenne pepper. Heat to boiling; reduce heat. Boil gently, uncovered, about 2 hours or until mixture is about the thickness of ketchup, stirring occasionally.

2 Ladle hot chili sauce into hot, sterilized half-pint canning jars, leaving a 1/2-inch headspace. Wipe jar rims; adjust lids. Process filled jars in a boiling-water canner for 15 minutes (start timing when water returns to boil). Remove jars from canner; cool on wire racks.

PER 1-TABLESPOON SERVING: 13 cal., 0 g total fat, 0 mg chol., 50 mg sodium, 3 g carbo., 1 g fiber, 0 g pro.

A summer fruit (peaches) and a fall fruit (pears) pair up with lip-tingling chiles in this sweet and spicy sauce. Try it on grilled chicken or turkey.

PEACH AND PEAR CHILI SAUCE

PREP: 45 MINUTES **COOK:** 2 HOURS **PROCESS:** 15 MINUTES **MAKES:** 4 PINTS (28 SERVINGS)

4 ½   **pounds tomatoes**

4   **medium pears, peeled, cored, and cut into ½-inch chunks (4 cups)**

4   **medium peaches, peeled, pitted, and cut into ½-inch chunks (3 ½ cups)**

2 ¼   **cups chopped green sweet peppers (3 medium)**

2   **cups chopped onions (4 medium)**

¾   **cup chopped red sweet pepper (1 medium)**

1   **to 2 red or green fresh serrano chile peppers, seeded and finely chopped (1 to 3 teaspoons)***

3   **cups sugar**

1 ½   **cups cider vinegar**

4   **teaspoons salt**

2   **teaspoons ground nutmeg**

1   **teaspoon whole cloves**

6   **inches stick cinnamon**

❶ Wash tomatoes. Remove peels, stem ends, and cores. Cut tomatoes into chunks (you should have 6¾ cups). In a 6- or 8-quart stainless-steel, enamel, or nonstick kettle or pot combine tomatoes, pears, peaches, green sweet peppers, onions, red sweet pepper, and chile peppers. Stir in sugar, vinegar, salt, and nutmeg.

❷ For a spice bag, place cloves and cinnamon on a double thickness of 6-inch-square pieces of 100-percent-cotton cheesecloth. Bring corners together and tie with clean kitchen string. Add spice bag to vegetable mixture. Heat to boiling; reduce heat. Simmer, uncovered, about 2 hours or until thick, stirring occasionally.

❸ Discard spice bag. Ladle hot chili sauce into hot, sterilized pint canning jars, leaving a ½-inch headspace. (Refrigerate any extra sauce; use within 3 days.) Wipe jar rims; adjust lids. Process filled jars in a boiling-water canner for 15 minutes (start timing when water returns to boil). Remove jars from canner; cool on wire racks.

*NOTE: Because chile peppers contain oils that can burn skin and eyes, avoid direct contact with them as much as possible. Wear plastic or rubber gloves while preparing them. If your bare hands should touch a chile pepper, wash well with soap and water.

PER ¼-CUP SERVING: 116 cal., 0 g total fat, 0 mg chol., 300 mg sodium, 29 g carbo., 2 g fiber, 1 g pro.

If you love garlic, you'll love this tomato and herb sauce packed full of it. Even better, the garlic is roasted first to give it a full, mellow flavor.

ROASTED GARLIC PASTA SAUCE

PREP: 2 ½ HOURS **BAKE:** 40 MINUTES **OVEN:** 400°F **COOK:** 60 MINUTES **PROCESS:** 35 MINUTES **MAKES:** 6 PINTS (11 CUPS)

6   **bulbs garlic**

3   **tablespoons olive oil**

4   **medium red, yellow, and/or green sweet peppers, halved and seeded**

12   **pounds ripe tomatoes (about 25 tomatoes), peeled (see page 34)**

3   **tablespoons packed brown sugar**

2   **tablespoons kosher salt or 4 teaspoons salt**

1   **tablespoon balsamic vinegar**

1   **teaspoon freshly ground black pepper**

2   **cups lightly packed fresh basil leaves, chopped**

1   **cup lightly packed assorted fresh herbs (such as oregano, thyme, parsley, flat-leaf parsley, or basil), chopped**

6   **tablespoons lemon juice**

1 Preheat oven to 400°F. Peel away dry outer layers of skin from garlic bulbs, leaving skins and cloves intact. Cut off ½ inch from pointed portions, leaving bulbs intact. Place garlic bulbs, cut sides up, in a small casserole. Drizzle with 1 tablespoon of the olive oil. Cover casserole. Arrange peppers, cut sides down, on a foil-lined baking sheet; brush with remaining 2 tablespoons olive oil. Bake garlic and peppers 40 to 50 minutes or until pepper skins are charred and cloves of garlic are soft. Cool garlic on a wire rack until cool enough to handle. Pull up sides of foil and pinch together to fully enclose peppers. Let stand 15 to 20 minutes or until cool enough to handle.

2 Remove garlic cloves from skins by squeezing bottoms of bulbs. Place cloves in a food processor. Cut tomatoes into chunks and add some chunks to food processor with garlic. Cover and process until chopped. Transfer chopped garlic and tomatoes to a 7- to 8-quart stainless-steel, enamel, or nonstick heavy kettle or pot. Chop remaining tomatoes, in batches, in food processor. Add to the pot.

3 Add brown sugar, salt, vinegar, and black pepper to tomato mixture. Heat to boiling. Boil steadily, uncovered, for 50 minutes, stirring occasionally. When peppers are cool enough to handle, peel off skins. Chop peppers. Add peppers to tomato mixture. Boil for 10 to 20 minutes more or until mixture is reduced to desired consistency, stirring occasionally. Remove from heat; stir in herbs.

4 Spoon 1 tablespoon lemon juice into hot, sterilized pint canning jars. Ladle hot sauce into jars with lemon juice, leaving a ½-inch headspace. Wipe the jar rims; adjust lids. Process filled jars in a boiling-water canner for 35 minutes (start timing when water returns to boil). Remove jars from canner; cool on wire racks.

PER ½ CUP SAUCE: 95 cal., 3 g total fat (0 g sat. fat), 0 mg chol., 542 mg sodium, 17 g carbo., 4 g fiber, 3 g pro.

This Midwestern favorite is delectable on ice cream or drizzled over pound cake or angel food cake, plain cheesecake, and bread pudding.

RHUBARB SAUCE

PREP: 10 MINUTES **COOK:** 5 MINUTES **PROCESS:** 5 MINUTES
MAKES: 4 HALF-PINTS (24 SERVINGS)

1 to 1 1/3 cups sugar

1/2 cup water

2 4×1-inch strip orange peel (optional)

6 cups sliced fresh or frozen rhubarb (about 2 pounds)

2 to 4 drops red food coloring (optional)

1 In a large saucepan stir together sugar, water, and, if using, orange peel. Heat to boiling; stir in rhubarb. Return to boiling; reduce heat. Simmer, covered, for 5 to 6 minutes or until rhubarb is tender. Remove from heat. Remove the orange peel, if using. If using fresh rhubarb, stir in food coloring if desired.

2 Ladle hot sauce into hot, sterilized half-pint canning jars, leaving a ½-inch headspace. Wipe jar rims; adjust lids. Process in a boiling-water canner for 5 minutes (start timing when water returns to boil). Remove jars from canner; cool on wire racks.

PER 2 -TABLESPOON SERVING: 39 cal., 0 g total fat, 0 mg chol., 1 mg sodium, 10 g carbo., 1 g fiber, 0 g pro.

Do you fancy other flavors of fruit syrup? Try raspberries or blackberries instead of strawberries.

STRAWBERRY SYRUP

PREP: 30 MINUTES **COOK:** 30 MINUTES **PROCESS:** 5 MINUTES **MAKES:** 4 HALF-PINTS (56 SERVINGS)

12 **cups strawberries**

2 **cups water**

3 **cups sugar**

❶ Wash berries; remove green caps. Place about half the berries in a large kettle. Use a slotted spoon or potato masher to crush berries in the kettle; add remaining berries and crush again. Add water. Heat to boiling; reduce heat. Cook, uncovered, over low heat for 5 minutes, stirring occasionally.

❷ Line a strainer or colander with a double layer of 100-percent-cotton cheesecloth; set over a bowl. Pour berry mixture into strainer. Press to drain all juice. Discard berry pulp. Measure 6 cups juice.

❸ In a 3- or 4-quart saucepan or kettle heat the juice to a rolling boil; stir in the sugar. Continue boiling about 30 minutes or until mixture is slightly thickened, stirring occasionally to prevent sticking.

❹ Pour syrup into hot, sterilized half-pint canning jars, leaving a ¼-inch headspace. Wipe jar rims; adjust lids. Process filled jars in boiling-water canner for 5 minutes (start timing when water returns to boil). Remove jars from canner; cool on wire racks.

PER 1-TABLESPOON SERVING: 51 cal., 0 g total fat, 0 mg chol., 1 mg sodium, 13 g carbo., 1 g fiber, 0 g pro.

Chapter Five

JAMS, JELLIES & PRESERVES

If you've never canned before, jams and other spreads are a good place to begin. They're fast to make and so absolutely delicious that you might want to lick the pan. They are universally loved, making homemade preserves a treasured gift.

MAKING YOUR OWN JAMS, JELLIES, AND PRESERVES

The full, fresh flavor of homemade preserves can't be replicated in mass-produced versions. Try your hand at a simple freezer jam to enjoy at home in minutes or concoct a rich, complex conserve to give as an elegant gift.

Whether you want a beautiful jar of peach jam to brighten breakfast or a delicious grape jelly to treat the kids after school, homemade preserves are among the most rewarding to make.

They're easy (especially freezer types) and beloved by young and old alike.

TIPS FOR THE BEST JAMS AND JELLIES

Choose fruits at the peak of their flavor and ripeness. Discard any berries with even a small spot of mildew—it might be tasted through the whole batch of preserves.

Make the amount specified in the recipe. Don't double or there may be problems with jelling or scorching in the pan.

Use the amount of sugar specified; don't alter. Sugar interacts with pectin to create an ideal texture. It also acts as a preservative and develops flavors.

Acid is needed for jelling and flavor. With low-acid fruits, follow the recipe, which will probably add lemon juice or citric acid.

TYPES OF PRESERVES

Different cooking methods and ingredients combine to make a variety of preserves:

Ⓐ CHUTNEY A staple in Indian and similar ethnic cuisines, chutneys are usually fruit-based (but can include vegetables too) and are highly spiced, often with hot pepper. Most recipes add some vinegar to make them piquant. While a few chutneys are sweet, most are best suited to savory foods.

JAMS, JELLIES AND PRESERVES TROUBLESHOOTING

PROBLEM	CAUSE	SOLUTION
Contains crystals.	The amount of sugar or cooking time may have been off or the method was wrong.	Measure sugar and other ingredients precisely. Cook traditional jams the specified time. Cooking too little doesn't allow sugar to dissolve; cooking too long results in too much evaporation. If sugar crystals stick to side of the pan during cooking, carefully wipe them off before filling jars.
Too soft or runny.	Pectin, which interacts with natural and added sugar and acid, was not allowed to develop properly.	Measure sugar, pectin, and other ingredients precisely. Do not double recipes for jams and jellies. Fruit may have been overripe with too much natural sugar. If cooked, the preserve may not have been boiled long enough at a rolling boil. (See page 158 for a thickness test.)
Contains bubbles.	Spoilage or trapped air	If bubbles are moving when the jar is still, the preserve has spoiled and should be discarded. If the bubbles are not moving when the jar is still, it was not ladled quickly enough into the jar. Also, pour the jam on the rim of the ladle, rather than directly into the jar, to prevent bubbles.
Mold occurs during storage.	Too much headspace or improper processing	Never use a wax seal with preserves. This outdated method encourages spoilage. Process in a boiling-water canner instead. Leave a ¼-inch headspace with preserves. Measure carefully. Process for the time specified in a current, reliable recipe.

B JAM Made by cooking crushed or chopped fruits with sugar until the proper thick consistency. Chunks of fruit are usually desirable. Firm but spreadable, a jam does not hold the shape of the jar.

C JELLY Made with the juice of one or more fruits, jelly is ideally very clear and firm. The pectin is concentrated enough that a good jelly, when the jar is dipped into hot water, unmolds onto a plate and keeps its shape. However, it also needs to be somewhat spreadable.

D MARMALADE Made as a soft, transparent jelly with bits of fruit or peel suspended in it. Most marmalades are citrus-based, as with orange marmalade—the most popular.

E FRUIT BUTTER Made by cooking pureed fruit or a pulp into a thick consistency. Spices, especially cinnamon, are often added. Cook slowly until the butter can mound on a spoon. Serve like a jam.

F CONSERVE Similar to a jam, but with a combination of fruits, nuts, and often raisins. Some are suitable for spreading like a jam on muffins and other breads. Others are more savory and are good to serve alongside grilled or roasted meats, such as turkey or pork, or with cheese.

TRADITIONAL JAMS call for ladling cooked jam into hot jars, sealing with lids, and then processing in a boiling-water canner.

C JELLY
Translucent and very firm with no bits of fruit

A CHUTNEY
A sweet-sour and savory combination of fruit, spices, and often a little vinegar

D MARMALADE
Usually a clear citrus spread with strips of peel

E FRUIT BUTTER
Thick and rich, made from a fruit puree

B JAM
Chunks of fruits in a semiclear spread

F CONSERVE
A chunky combination of fresh fruits, nuts, and often dried fruits

HOW TO MAKE TRADITIONAL JAM

Traditional jams are cooked in a pot to thicken and to break down the fruit. They are then poured into jars and processed in a canner. To make a traditional jam:

❶ Wash the fruit thoroughly and prepare as directed in the recipe. In this example, remove the hulls from the strawberries.

❷ Mash or puree the fruit as directed in the recipe. In most cases a potato masher is the best tool for this job.

❸ Measure the pureed fruit into a large pan along with the sugar, any pectin specified in the recipe, and flavorings.

❹ Bring to a full, rolling boil, critical in jellymaking. (Don't fill the pan more than one-third full or it may boil over.)

❺ The mixture will sheet off a spoon when it has reached its jelling point. To test, dip a metal spoon into the boiling mixture and hold over the pan. If the mixture is ready, 2 drops will hang off the spoon, then run together in a sheetlike action. Or use a candy thermometer to achieve the jelling point—220°F at sea level.

❻ Boiling naturally results in foam. Skim it off with spoon.

❼ Then fill hot, sterilized jars as directed in the recipe, leaving a ¼-inch headspace. Wipe jar rims, adjust lids, and process in a boiling-water canner (see page 36).

THE ROLE OF PECTIN

Pectin is a thickening agent found in nature that gives jams, jellies, and other preserves their desired texture.

Some fruits are naturally high in pectin, including apples, gooseberries, limes, lemons, cranberries, and red currants. Recipes that include high-pectin fruits may not call for additional pectin.

However, with lower-pectin fruits, such as raspberries, rhubarb, and cherries, pectin must be added or the resulting preserves would be runny.

It used to be that only a traditional powdered pectin was available. Today several types are available to fit a variety of recipes.

Use the pectin called for in the recipe. Do not substitute a different type.

TRADITIONAL POWDERED PECTIN: For regular preserves recipes. Must be cooked.

LIQUID PECTIN: Already dissolved, so mixes in easily. Often used in freezer jams.

NO-SUGAR PECTIN: The only pectin to use for reduced- or no-sugar jams because sugar affects how well pectin works.

FREEZER JAM PECTIN: Made specifically to dissolve easily and gel well in no-cook preserves recipes.

HOW TO MAKE FREEZER AND MICROWAVE JAM

FREEZER JAM

Freezer jam, sometimes called easy jam, is indeed simple. Just mash fruit, add pectin, sugar, and other flavorings.

Here's how to make it:

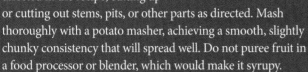

1 Choose perfectly ripe fruit. Wash thoroughly. Prepare fruit as directed in the recipe, cutting up or cutting out stems, pits, or other parts as directed. Mash thoroughly with a potato masher, achieving a smooth, slightly chunky consistency that will spread well. Do not puree fruit in a food processor or blender, which would make it syrupy.

2 Add the pectin. (Liquid pectin is shown here.) Powdered pectins are sometimes mixed with sugar first before adding. Add other ingredients and flavorings as directed in the recipe. Stir the fruit mixture for the time specified in the recipe. This helps develop the pectin for the best texture.

3 Wash clean plastic freezer jars, glass jelly jars, plastic freezer containers, or other freezer-proof container. Ladle jam into containers, allowing a ¼-inch headspace. Cover and label. Allow to set up for 24 hours, or freeze. Before serving, thaw for several hours in the refrigerator.

MICROWAVE JAM

The simplest jam to make, hands down, is microwave jam. It's so easy, you can make it in the morning to serve for breakfast that same day.

The only catch to making microwave jam is that you need to start with a microwave recipe. The process involves cooking mashed fruit and sugar in the microwave, sometimes with the addition of lemon or butter to prevent foaming. Most micro-wave recipes are for small batches. Don't adapt other recipes to this method—and don't double it. Make the recipe just as it's written and enjoy.

After preparing the jam, let it cool and thicken in the refrigerator before serving. Store for up to a week.

There are few things more sweetly satisfying on a January morning than biting into a crispy piece of warm toast, slathered with jam made with perfectly ripe berries that you picked in June.

STRAWBERRY JAM

PREP: 35 MINUTES **PROCESS:** 5 MINUTES **MAKES:** ABOUT 7 HALF-PINTS

3 **quarts fresh strawberries, hulled**

1 **1.75-ounce package regular powdered fruit pectin**

½ **teaspoon butter**

7 **cups sugar**

❶ Place 1 cup of berries in an 8-quart heavy kettle or pot. Use a potato masher to crush berries. Continue adding berries and crushing them until you have 5 cups crushed berries. Stir in pectin and butter. Bring to a full rolling boil, stirring constantly.

❷ Add sugar all at once. Return to a full rolling boil; boil for 1 minute, stirring constantly. Remove from heat; skim off foam with a metal spoon.

❸ Ladle immediately into hot, sterilized half-pint canning jars, leaving a ¼-inch headspace. Wipe jar rims; adjust lids. Process filled jars in a boiling-water canner for 5 minutes (start timing when water returns to boil). (See page 191 for timing adjustments based on altitude.) Remove jars from canner; cool on wire racks.*

*NOTE: As the jam cools, turn the jars occasionally, top to bottom, to help evenly distribute the fruit and prevent the fruit from floating to the top of the jars. Store upright, however, to protect the seal.

PER 1-TABLESPOON SERVING: 51 cal., 0 g total fat), 0 mg chol., 1 mg sodium, 13 g carbo., 0 g fiber, 0 g pro.

Dark sweet cherries and a hint of lemon add up to a sensational spread. A cherry pitter, available from a cookware shop or catalog, removes pits from cherries easily. Or halve the cherries and then pop out the pits with the tip of a knife.

SWEET CHERRY JAM

PREP: 35 MINUTES **PROCESS:** 5 MINUTES **MAKES:** 6 HALF-PINTS (84 SERVINGS)

3 **pounds fully ripe dark sweet cherries**

1 **1.75-ounce package regular powdered fruit pectin**

1 **teaspoon finely shredded lemon peel**

¼ **cup lemon juice**

5 **cups sugar**

❶ Sort, wash, stem, pit, and chop cherries. Measure 4 cups chopped cherries.

❷ In a 6- or 8-quart kettle or pot combine cherries, pectin, lemon peel, and lemon juice. Heat over high heat until mixture comes to a boil, stirring constantly. Stir in sugar. Bring to a full rolling boil. Boil for 1 minute, stirring constantly. Remove from heat. Quickly skim off foam with a metal spoon.

❸ Ladle at once into hot, sterilized half-pint canning jars, leaving a ¼-inch headspace. Wipe jar rims; adjust lids. Process filled jars in a boiling-water canner for 5 minutes (start timing when water returns to boil). (See page 191 for timing adjustments based on altitude.) Remove jars from canner; cool on wire racks.

PER 1-TABLESPOON SERVING: 58 cal., 0 g total fat, 0 mg chol., 1 mg sodium, 15 g carbo., 0 g fiber, 0 g pro.

Raspberries are easy to grow in your backyard and the brambles spread over time, producing loads of jewellike berries. Savor their flavor in this gorgeous jam.

RASPBERRY JAM

PREP: 35 MINUTES **PROCESS:** 5 MINUTES **MAKES:** 8 HALF-PINTS (112 SERVINGS)

2 **quarts fresh raspberries**

1 **1.75-ounce package regular powdered fruit pectin**

7 **cups sugar**

1 Place 1 cup of the berries in an 8-quart kettle or pot; crush berries. Continue adding berries and crushing them until you have 5 cups crushed berries. Stir in pectin. Heat over high heat, stirring constantly, until mixture comes to a full rolling boil. Add sugar all at once. Return to full rolling boil; boil for 1 minute, stirring constantly. Remove from heat; skim off foam with a metal spoon.

2 Immediately ladle jam into hot, sterilized half-pint canning jars, leaving a ¼-inch headspace. Wipe jar rims; adjust lids. Process filled jars in a boiling-water canner for 5 minutes (start timing when the water returns to boil). (See page 191 for timing adjustments based on altitude.) Remove jars from canner; cool on wire rack.

TEST KITCHEN TIP: To reduce sweetness of the jam, add 2 tablespoons lemon juice to the fruit mixture before processing.

TEST KITCHEN TIP: Jazz up a basic fruit jam such as this one by adding one of the following to the fruit mixture along with the sugar: 1 teaspoon finely shredded lemon peel, ½ teaspoon ground nutmeg, or ¼ teaspoon grated fresh ginger.

PER 1-TABLESPOON SERVING: 46 cal., 0 g total fat, 0 mg chol., 1 mg sodium, 12 g carbo., 1 g fiber, 0 g pro.

Enhance the subtle flavor of blueberries with a hint of cinnamon, allspice, and cloves. For classic blueberry jam, simply omit them.

SPICED BLUEBERRY JAM

PREP: 30 MINUTES **PROCESS:** 6 MINUTES **MAKES:** 9 HALF-PINTS (126 SERVINGS)

6 **cups blueberries**

2 **tablespoons lemon juice**

½ **teaspoon ground cinnamon**

¼ **teaspoon ground allspice**

Dash ground cloves

7 **cups sugar**

1 **6-ounce package (2 foil pouches) liquid fruit pectin**

1 Crush blueberries with a potato masher. (You should have 4½ cups crushed berries.) In an 8- or 10-quart kettle or pot combine crushed blueberries, lemon juice, cinnamon, allspice, and cloves. Stir in sugar.

2 Heat over high heat to a full rolling boil, stirring constantly. Stir in pectin. Return to a full rolling boil. Boil hard for 1 minute, stirring constantly. Remove from heat; skim off foam with a metal spoon.

3 Ladle at once into hot, sterilized half-pint jars, leaving a ¼-inch headspace. Wipe jar rims; adjust lids. Process filled jars in a boiling-water canner for 5 minutes (start timing when water returns to boil). (See page 191 for timing adjustments based on altitude.) Remove jars from canner; cool in wire racks.

PER 1-TABLESPOON SERVING : 41 cal., 0 g total fat, 0 mg chol., 1 mg sodium, 11 g carbo., 0 g pro.

Use only Concord grapes for this jam; other grapes will not work. Fortunately, Concords are easy to grow and the vines last for decades. If you don't have them growing in your yard, a friend or neighbor might. Otherwise, look for them at farmers' markets.

GRAPE JAM

PREP: 65 MINUTES **COOK:** 40 MINUTES **PROCESS:** 5 MINUTES **MAKES:** 6 HALF-PINTS (84 SERVINGS)

3 ½   pounds Concord grapes

2   cups water

4 ½   cups sugar

❶ Wash and stem grapes. Measure 8 cups. Remove skins from half of the grapes; set aside.

❷ In an 8- or 10-quart heavy kettle or pot combine the skinned and unskinned grapes. Cover and cook about 10 minutes or until very soft. Press grapes through a sieve; discard seeds and cooked skins. Measure 3 cups of strained pulp; return to kettle. Stir in the uncooked grape skins and water. Cook, covered, for 10 minutes. Uncover; stir in sugar. Bring mixture to a full rolling boil, stirring often. Boil, uncovered, for 18 to 24 minutes or until jam sheets off a metal spoon (see page 159).

❸ Remove kettle from heat; quickly skim off foam with a metal spoon.

❹ Immediately ladle jam into hot, sterilized half-pint canning jars, leaving a ¼-inch headspace. Wipe jar rims; adjust lids. Process in a boiling-water canner for 5 minutes (start timing when water returns to boil). (See page 191 for timing adjustments based on altitude.) Remove jars from canner; cool on wire racks.

PER 1-TABLESPOON SERVING: 46 cal., 0 g total fat, 0 mg chol., 0 mg sodium, 12 g carbo., 0 g fiber, 0 g pro.

You can use a variety of figs for this recipe—Black Mission figs or golden Calimyrna figs work equally well. Spread the jam on crackers and serve with blue cheese—or use it as a filling for buttery cookies.

FIG JAM

PREP: 50 MINUTES **PROCESS:** 5 MINUTES **MAKES:** 10 HALF-PINTS (160 SERVINGS)

2 ¾   **pounds fresh Black Mission figs (30 to 35)**

¾   **cup bottled lemon juice**

⅓   **cup water**

1   **1.75 -ounce package powdered fruit pectin**

7   **cups sugar**

① Rinse figs. Remove stems from figs; halve or quarter figs. Place one-third of the figs in a food processor or one-sixth in a blender. Cover; process or blend until almost smooth (you should have some finely chopped pieces, not pureed fruit). Transfer fruit to a large bowl. Repeat with remaining figs. Measure 5 cups fig pulp.

② In an 8-quart heavy kettle or pot stir together the fig pulp, the lemon juice, water, and pectin. Heat over high heat, stirring constantly, until mixture comes to a full rolling boil. Add sugar all at once. Return to full rolling boil; boil for 1 minute, stirring constantly. Remove from heat; skim off foam with a metal spoon.

③ Immediately ladle jam into hot, sterilized half-pint canning jars, leaving a ¼-inch headspace. Wipe jar rims; adjust lids. Process filled jars in a boiling-water canner for 5 minutes (start timing when water returns to boil). (See page 191 for timing adjustments based on altitude.) Remove jars from canner; cool on wire racks.

PER 1-TABLESPOON SERVING: 45 cal., 0 g total fat, 0 mg chol., 1 mg sodium, 12 g carbo., 0 g fiber, 0 g pro.

For the most intense citrusy flavor and best texture, allow the marmalade to set up to 2 weeks before sampling this sweet-tart spread.

ORANGE MARMALADE

PREP: 55 MINUTES **COOK:** 30 MINUTES **PROCESS:** 5 MINUTES
MAKES: 6 HALF-PINTS (96 SERVINGS)

4	medium oranges
1	medium lemon
1½	cups water
⅛	teaspoon baking soda
5	cups sugar
½	of a 6-ounce package (1 foil pouch) liquid fruit pectin

❶ Score orange and lemon peels into 4 lengthwise sections; remove the peels with your fingers. Scrape off the bitter white portions and discard; cut peels into thin strips. In a medium saucepan combine peels, water, and baking soda. Bring to boiling; reduce heat. Simmer, covered, for 20 minutes. Do not drain.

❷ Section fruits, reserving juices; discard seeds. Add fruits and juices to peels; return to boiling. Simmer, covered, for 10 minutes. Measure 3 cups.

❸ In an 8- to 10-quart heavy kettle or pot combine fruit mixture and sugar. Bring to a full rolling boil, stirring constantly. Quickly stir in pectin. Return to a full rolling boil; boil for 1 minute, stirring constantly. Remove from heat; skim off foam with a metal spoon.

❹ Immediately ladle marmalade into hot, sterilized half-pint canning jars, leaving a ¼-inch headspace. Wipe jar rims; adjust lids. Process in a boiling-water canner for 5 minutes (start timing when water returns to boil). (See page 191 for timing adjustments based on altitude.) Remove jars from canner; cool on wire racks.

PER 1-TABLESPOON SERVING: 46 cal., 0 g total fat, 0 mg chol., 2 mg sodium, 12 g carbo., 0 g fiber, 0 g pro.

Cranberries, orange, and brandy are familiar holiday flavors, making this the quintessential preserve to share as a seasonal gift. But be sure to make plenty for yourself too. You'll want to have it on hand all year.

BRANDIED CRANBERRY-ORANGE MARMALADE

PREP: 65 MINUTES **COOK:** 30 MINUTES **PROCESS:** 5 MINUTES **STAND:** 3 DAYS
MAKES: ABOUT 6 HALF-PINTS (96 SERVINGS)

3	medium oranges
1½	cups water
⅛	teaspoon baking soda
2	cups fresh cranberries
4	inches stick cinnamon
4	cups sugar
½	of a 6-ounce package (1 foil pouch) liquid fruit pectin
2	tablespoons brandy

❶ Score orange peels into 4 lengthwise sections; remove the peels with your fingers. Scrape off the bitter white portions and discard; cut peels into extremely thin strips. In a medium saucepan combine peels, water, and baking soda. Bring to boiling; reduce heat. Simmer, covered, for 20 minutes. Do not drain.

❷ Section oranges, reserving juices; discard seeds. Add orange sections, juice, cranberries, and cinnamon to peels; return to boiling. Simmer, covered, for 10 minutes. Discard stick cinnamon.

❸ In an 8- to 10-quart heavy kettle or pot combine fruit mixture and sugar. Bring to a full rolling boil, stirring constantly. Quickly stir in pectin. Return to a full rolling boil; boil for 1 minute, stirring constantly. Remove from heat; skim off foam with a metal spoon. Stir in brandy.

❹ Immediately ladle marmalade into hot, sterilized half-pint canning jars, leaving a ¼-inch headspace. Wipe jar rims; adjust lids. Process filled jars in a boiling-water canner for 5 minutes (start timing when water returns to boil). (See page 191 for timing adjustments based on altitude.) Remove jars from canner; cool on racks. Let marmalade stand for 3 to 5 days before serving to allow flavors to blend.

PER 1-TABLESPOON SERVING: 36 cal., 0 g total fat, 0 mg chol., 2 mg sodium, 9 g carbo., 0 g fiber, 0 g pro.

Grapes in this jelly should be at two stages of ripeness. Less-ripe grapes contribute more pectin, helping the jelly to set. More-ripe grapes lend a richer, fuller flavor.

OLD-FASHIONED GRAPE JELLY

PREP: 45 MINUTES **COOK:** 30 MINUTES **STAND:** 4 ½ HOURS **CHILL:** 12 TO 14 HOURS **PROCESS:** 5 MINUTES **MAKES:** 5 HALF-PINTS (70 SERVINGS)

6 **pounds Concord grapes (use about 4 ½ pounds fully ripe grapes and about 1 ½ pounds firm, slightly less-ripe grapes)**

¾ **cup water**

3 ¾ **cups sugar**

1 Wash and stem grapes. In a 6- to 8-quart kettle or pot crush grapes with a potato masher. Add the water. Bring to boiling over high heat; reduce heat. Simmer, covered, about 10 minutes or until grapes are very soft.

2 Using a jelly bag or a colander lined with several layers of 100-percent-cotton cheesecloth, strain the mixture. (This will take about 4½ hours.) You should have about 7 cups of juice. Refrigerate the juice for 12 to 14 hours. Strain again through the clean jelly bag or cheesecloth, being careful to strain out sediment.

3 Place juice in the same kettle. Add sugar; stir to dissolve. Bring to a full rolling boil. Boil hard, uncovered, until syrup sheets off a metal spoon or reaches 220°F. This will take about 20 minutes. Remove from heat. Quickly skim off foam with a metal spoon.

4 Immediately ladle jelly into hot, sterilized half-pint canning jars, leaving a ¼-inch headspace. Wipe jar rims; adjust lids. Process filled jars in a boiling-water canner for 5 minutes (start timing when water returns to boil). (See page 191 for timing adjustments based on altitude.) Remove jars from canner; cool on wire racks.

PER 1-TABLESPOON SERVING: 52 cal., 0 g total fat, 0 g chol., 0 mg sodium, 14 g carbo., 1 g fiber, 0 g pro.

Because this recipe starts with fruit juice, it goes together quickly and easily yet has the great taste of homemade jelly. If you like, substitute other 100-percent fruit juice blends for the suggested juices.

FRUIT JUICE JELLY

PREP: 25 MINUTES **PROCESS:** 5 MINUTES **MAKES:** 5 HALF-PINTS (80 SERVINGS)

4 cups cranberry juice (not low-calorie) or unsweetened apple, grape, or orange juice

¼ cup bottled lemon juice

1 1.75-ounce package regular powdered fruit pectin

4½ cups sugar

1 Pour fruit juice and lemon juice into a 6- to 8-quart heavy kettle or pot. Sprinkle with pectin. Let stand for 1 to 2 minutes; stir to dissolve. Bring to a full rolling boil over medium-high heat, stirring frequently. Stir in sugar. Return to a full rolling boil, stirring frequently. Boil hard for 1 minute, stirring constantly. Remove from heat; quickly skim off foam with a metal spoon.

2 Ladle jelly at once into hot, sterilized half-pint canning jars, leaving a ¼-inch headspace. Wipe jar rims; adjust lids. Process filled jars in a boiling-water canner for 5 minutes (start timing when water returns to boil). (See page 191 for timing adjustments based on altitude.) Remove jars from canner; cool on wire racks until set.

PER 1-TABLESPOON SERVING: 68 cal., 0 g total fat, 0 mg chol., 2 mg sodium, 18 g carbo., 0 g fiber, 0 g pro.

Savor fresh herbs year-round in flavorful jelly. Start with your favorite herb for the first batch—mint is a classic—then try others. Serve on toast, with rolls at dinner, or as a sweet complement to chicken, lamb, and other meats.

HERB JELLY

PREP: 40 MINUTES **STAND:** 10 MINUTES **PROCESS:** 5 MINUTES **MAKES:** 5 HALF-PINTS (80 SERVINGS)

2 **to 3 ounces freshly picked herb sprigs and/or edible flower petals (one or more types according to taste)**

3 **cups unsweetened apple juice**

¼ **cup bottled lemon juice**

1 **1.75-ounce package regular powdered fruit pectin**

Few drops yellow food coloring (optional)

4 **cups sugar**

❶ Gently wash herb sprigs and/or flower petals in water. Drain; place on paper towels and gently blot. Chop herbs with stems attached. Measure 1 to 1½ cups firmly packed leaves and stems or flower petals; transfer to an 8- to 10-quart heavy kettle or pot. Add apple juice.

❷ Bring to boiling over high heat. Boil, uncovered, for 5 minutes. Remove from heat. Cover and let stand for 10 minutes.

❸ Line a strainer or colander with a double layer of 100-percent-cotton cheesecloth. Strain herb and/or flower mixture through cheesecloth, pressing to extract all juice. Measure juice mixture; if necessary, add enough additional apple juice to equal 3 cups. Discard stems, leaves, and petals.

❹ In the same kettle combine the apple juice mixture, lemon juice, fruit pectin, and, if desired, food coloring. Bring to a full rolling boil over medium-high heat, stirring constantly. Add sugar all at once. Return to full rolling boil; boil for 1 minute, stirring constantly. Remove from heat; quickly skim off foam with a metal spoon.

❺ Ladle jelly at once into hot, sterilized half-pint canning jars, leaving a ¼-inch headspace. Wipe jar rims; adjust lids. Process filled jars in a boiling-water canner for 5 minutes (start timing when water returns to boil). (See page 191 for timing adjustments based on altitude.) Remove jars from canner; cool on wire racks.

PER 1-TABLESPOON SERVING: 44 cal., 0 g total fat, 0 mg chol., 2 mg sodium, 11 g carbo., 0 g fiber, 0 g pro.

Try this lively jelly over cream cheese with crackers, on goat cheese crostini, or as a side to plain grilled or roasted meats. Choose your hotness level by using two, three, or four jalapeños.

JALAPEÑO PEPPER JELLY

PREP: 50 MINUTES **PROCESS:** 5 MINUTES **MAKES:** 5 HALF-PINTS (70 SERVINGS)

1½   cups cranberry juice (not low-calorie)

1   cup vinegar

2   to 4 fresh jalapeño chile peppers, halved, and, if desired, seeded*

5   cups sugar

½   of a 6-ounce package (1 foil pouch) liquid fruit pectin

5   tiny hot red peppers

1 In a medium stainless-steel, enamel, or nonstick saucepan combine cranberry juice, vinegar, and jalapeño peppers. Bring to boiling; reduce heat. Simmer, covered, for 10 minutes. Strain mixture through a sieve, pressing with the back of a spoon to remove all the liquid; measure 2 cups. Discard pulp.

2 In a heavy 6-quart kettle combine the 2 cups liquid and sugar. Bring to a full rolling boil over high heat, stirring constantly. Quickly stir in pectin and tiny hot red peppers. Return to a full rolling boil; boil for 1 minute, stirring constantly. Remove from heat. Quickly skim off foam with a metal spoon.

3 Ladle jelly at once into hot, sterilized half-pint jars, leaving a ¼-inch headspace and making sure each jar contains one tiny red pepper. Wipe jar rims; adjust lids. Process in a boiling-water canner for 5 minutes (start timing when water returns to boil). (See page 191 for timing adjustments based on altitude.) Remove jars from canner; cool on wire racks.

*NOTE: Because chile peppers contain oils that can burn skin and eyes, avoid direct contact with them as much as possible. Wear plastic or rubber gloves while preparing them. If your bare hands should touch a chile pepper, wash them well with soap and water.

PER 1-TABLESPOON SERVING: 57 cal., 0 g total fat, 0 mg chol., 0 mg sodium, 15 g carbo., 0 g fiber, 0 g pro.

The apples-and-spice aroma of this old-time favorite simmering on the stove is homey and welcoming—and the taste is pretty wonderful too. Spread this fruit butter on toasted English muffins or crumpets.

APPLE BUTTER

PREP: 45 MINUTES **COOK:** 2 HOURS **PROCESS:** 5 MINUTES **MAKES:** 6 HALF-PINTS (96 SERVINGS)

4 1/2 pounds tart cooking apples, cored and quartered (about 14 medium)

3 cups apple cider or apple juice

2 cups sugar

2 tablespoons fresh lemon juice, strained

1/2 teaspoon ground cinnamon

❶ In an 8- to 10-quart heavy kettle or pot combine apples and cider. Bring to boiling; reduce heat. Simmer, covered, for 30 minutes, stirring occasionally. Press through a food mill or sieve until you have 7½ cups. Return pulp to kettle.

❷ Stir in sugar, lemon juice, and cinnamon. Bring to boiling; reduce heat. Cook, uncovered, over very low heat for 1½ to 1¾ hours or until very thick and mixture mounds on a spoon, stirring often.

❸ Ladle hot apple butter into hot, sterilized half-pint canning jars, leaving a ¼-inch headspace. Wipe jar rims; adjust lids. Process in a boiling-water canner for 5 minutes (start timing when water returns to boil). (See page 191 for timing adjustments based on altitude.) Remove jars from canner; cool on wire racks.

PER 1-TABLESPOON SERVING: 28 cal., 0 g total fat, 0 mg chol., 0 mg sodium, 7 g carbo., 0 g fiber, 0 g pro.

APPLE-PEAR BUTTER: Prepare recipe as above, except substitute 2 pounds cored, quartered ripe pears for 2 pounds of the apples. Continue as directed.

CARAMEL APPLE BUTTER: Prepare recipe as above, except decrease granulated sugar to ½ cup and add 1½ cups packed brown sugar.

INDEX

ALTITUDE ADJUSTMENTS

The processing times in this book are based on conditions at 1,000 feet or less below sea level. When processing at high altitudes, adjust processing times.

Water boils at a higher temperature at higher altitudes, which means that when you are canning at higher elevations, you must process food longer to ensure that it is safe to eat when stored at room temperature.

What is the elevation where you live? You may be surprised at how high it is. Much of the flat Midwest, for example, is above 1,000 feet. Check your community's altitude online before you begin canning so you can adjust processing times appropriately according to the following guidelines.

BLANCHING: Add 1 minute if you live 5,000 feet or more above sea level.

BOILING-WATER CANNER: Call your county extension service for detailed instructions.

JELLIES AND JAMS: Add 1 minute of processing time for each additional 1,000 feet.

PRESSURE CANNING: Timings are the same, but different pressures must be used.

FOR DIAL-GAUGE PRESSURE CANNERS:

Feet above sea level	Pounds of pressure
Up to 2,000	11
2,001 to 4,000	12
4,001 to 6,000	13
6,001 to 8,000	14

FOR WEIGHTED-GAUGE CANNERS:

Feet above sea level	Pounds of pressure
Up to 1,000	10
Above 1,000	15

STERILIZING JARS: Boil jars an additional 1 minute for each additional 1,000 feet.

METRIC INFORMATION

These charts provide a guide for converting measurements from the U.S. customary system, which is used throughout this book, to the metric system.

PRODUCT DIFFERENCES

Most of the ingredients called for in the recipes in this book are available in most countries. However, some are known by different names. Here are some common American ingredients and their possible counterparts:
- Sugar (white) is granulated, fine granulated, or castor sugar.
- Green, red, or yellow sweet peppers are capsicums or bell peppers.
- Golden raisins are sultanas.

VOLUME AND WEIGHT

The United States traditionally uses cup measures for liquid and solid ingredients. The chart below shows the approximate imperial and metric equivalents. If you are accustomed to weighing solid ingredients, the following approximate equivalents will be helpful.
- Canadian and U.S. volume for a cup measure is 8 fluid ounces (237 ml), but the standard metric equivalent is 250 ml.
- 1 British imperial cup is 10 fluid ounces.
- In Australia, 1 tablespoon equals 20 ml, and there are 4 teaspoons in the Australian tablespoon.
- Spoon measures are used for smaller amounts of ingredients. Although the size of the tablespoon varies slightly in different countries, for practical purposes and for recipes in this book, a straight substitution is all that's necessary. Measurements made using cups or spoons always should be level unless stated otherwise.

COMMON WEIGHT RANGE REPLACEMENTS

Imperial / U.S.	Metric
¼ ounce	15 g
1 ounce	25 g or 30 g
4 ounces (¼ pound)	115 g or 125 g
8 ounces (½ pound)	225 g or 250 g
16 ounces (1 pound)	450 g or 500 g
1¼ pounds	625 g
1¼ pounds	750 g
2 pounds or 2¼ pounds	1,000 g or 1 Kg

OVEN TEMPERATURE EQUIVALENTS

Fahrenheit Setting	Celsius Setting	Gas Setting
300°F	150°C	Gas Mark 2 (very low)
325°F	160°C	Gas Mark 3 (low)
350°F	180°C	Gas Mark 4 (moderate)
375°F	190°C	Gas Mark 5 (moderate)
400°F	200°C	Gas Mark 6 (hot)
425°F	220°C	Gas Mark 7 (hot)
450°F	230°C	Gas Mark 8 (very hot)
475°F	240°C	Gas Mark 9 (very hot)
500°F	260°C	Gas Mark 10 (extremely hot)
Broil	Broil	Grill

*Electric and gas ovens may be calibrated using celsius. However, for an electric oven, increase celsius setting 10 to 20 degrees when cooking above 160°C. For convection or forced-air ovens (gas or electric), lower the temperature setting 25°F/10°C when cooking at all heat levels.

U.S. / STANDARD METRIC EQUIVALENTS

⅛ teaspoon = 0.5 ml
¼ teaspoon = 1 ml
½ teaspoon = 2 ml
1 teaspoon = 5 ml
1 tablespoon = 15 ml
2 tablespoons = 25 ml
¼ cup = 2 fluid ounces = 50 ml
⅓ cup = 3 fluid ounces = 75 ml
½ cup = 4 fluid ounces = 125 ml
⅔ cup = 5 fluid ounces = 150 ml
¾ cup = 6 fluid ounces = 175 ml
1 cup = 8 fluid ounces = 250 ml
2 cups = 1 pint = 500 ml
1 quart = 1 litre